182781

401.9
SOC

Social contexts of
messages

DATE			

© THE BAKER & TAYLOR CO.

SOCIAL CONTEXTS OF MESSAGES

European Monographs in Social Psychology
Editor: Henri Tajfel

IN PREPARATION

J. Israel and H. Tajfel
The Context of Social Psychology

M. von Cranach and I. Vine
Social Communication and Movement

W. Stroebe and J. R. Eiser
Categorization and Social Judgement

C. Herzlich
Health and Sickness: A Social Psychological Analysis

H. Giles and P. F. Powesland
Social Evaluation through Speech Characteristics

P. Weinreich
Theoretical and Experimental Evaluation of Dissonance Processes

E. Apfelbaum
Dynamic Processes in Interpersonal Conflict

EUROPEAN MONOGRAPHS IN SOCIAL PSYCHOLOGY **1**
Series Editor HENRI TAJFEL

SOCIAL CONTEXTS OF MESSAGES

Edited by

E. A. Carswell

Medical Research Council
Speech and Communication Research Unit,
University of Edinburgh, Scotland

Ragnar Rommetveit

Institute of Psychology
University of Oslo, Norway

1971

Published in co-operation with the

EUROPEAN ASSOCIATION OF
EXPERIMENTAL SOCIAL PSYCHOLOGY

by

ACADEMIC PRESS · LONDON AND NEW YORK

WITHDRAWN
LORETTE WILMOT LIBRARY
NAZARETH COLLEGE

ACADEMIC PRESS INC. (LONDON) LTD.
24–28 Oval Road
London, NW1 7DX

U.S. Edition published by
ACADEMIC PRESS INC.
111 Fifth Avenue,
New York, New York 10003

Copyright © 1971 By ACADEMIC PRESS INC. (LONDON) LTD

All Rights Reserved

No part of this book may be reproduced in any form by photostat, microfilm, or any other means, without written permission from the publishers

Library of Congress Catalog Card Number: 72-153534
ISBN: 0-12-161250-3

182781

PRINTED IN GREAT BRITAIN BY
THE WHITEFRIARS PRESS LTD., LONDON AND TONBRIDGE

LORETTE WILMOT LIBRARY
NAZARETH COLLEGE

401.9
Soc

CONTRIBUTORS

BLAKAR, R. M., *Psykologisk Instituit, Universitetet 1, Oslo, Norway*

CARSWELL, E. A., *Speech and Communication Unit, 31 Buccleuch Place, Edinburgh, Scotland*

COOK, M., *Institute of Experimental Psychology, University of Oxford, Oxford, England*

HAVELKA, N., *Department of Psychology, University of Belgrade, Draze Pavlovica 7, Belgrade, Yugoslavia*

HENRY, P., *Laboratoire de Psychologie Sociale, 54 Boulevard Raspail, Sorbonne, Paris VIᵉ, France*

HERKNER, W., *Psychologisches Institut der Universität Wien, 1010 Wien, Liebiggasse 5, Austria*

JASPARS, J., *Psychologisch Instituut, Rijksuniversiteit te Leiden, Rijnsburgerweg 169, Leiden, Netherlands*

KVALE, S., *Psykologisk Instituit, Universitetet 1, Oslo, Norway*

PÊCHEUX, M., *Laboratoire de Psychologie Sociale, 18 rue de la Sorbonne, Paris Vᵉ, France*

PEETERS, G., *Laboratoorium voor Experimentele Sociale Psychologie, Universiteit te Leuven, Belgium*

ROMMETVEIT, R., *Psykologisk Instituit, Universitetet 1, Oslo, Norway*

SKJERVE, J., *Psykologisk Instituit, Universitetet 1, Oslo, Norway*

WOLD, A. H., *Psykologisk Instituit, Universitetet 1, Oslo, Norway*

FOREWORD

It is fitting that the present monograph should be the first in the series of European Monographs in Social Psychology. It represents a convergence of scientific interests and of diverse backgrounds that, we hope, will remain characteristic of some of the monographs which will appear in the near future.

The initial planning of the monograph and the various stages of work which resulted in its publication were closely interwoven with the development of the European Association of Experimental Social Psychology which sponsors the series. As the editors write in their introduction, the idea of publishing the monograph first arose in connection with the work done at the second European Summer School in social psychology, held in Louvain in 1967, and organized in part by the European Association. Further stages of the preparation were greatly helped by individual "exchange visits" across Europe, also sponsored by the Association; and the subsequent conference in Oslo which enabled the authors to continue working together was supported jointly by the Norwegian Social Science Research Council and the Association. Equally important is the fact that the monograph represents by no means the end of the road. This Foreword is written only two weeks after another "small working group meeting" of the Association was held in Paris (with participants from Britain, France, the Netherlands, Norway and Rumania) on a theme closely related to that of the present monograph. In all these ways, the publication of the "Social Contexts of Messages" is like one strand among many, all having similar origins and composition. The origins are in the development of active exchange and cooperation amongst social psychologists in Europe; the "composition" consists of the ingredients of this cooperation, such as the summer schools, the exchange visits, the small working group meetings, the recent appearance of the first issue of the *European Journal of Social Psychology*; and perhaps, most of all, a new network of personal contacts and friendships across Europe.

Why a *European* Association and a series of *European* Monographs in Social Psychology? These titles are not meant to reflect some new version of "wider" or "continental" nationalism—academic, intellectual or any other. The future of social psychology as a discipline and as a contribution to knowledge and society is no more "European", "American" or "African" than it is Basque, Welsh, English, German or French. It is, however, true that the past and the present of what is often defined as the "scientific study of human social behaviour" are predominantly American. More work has been and is being done in the United States than in all the rest of the world together. This is so for a number of historical, social, economic and even political reasons which cannot be discussed in a brief note. In the long run such an exclusive focus from, and on, one cultural context cannot escape being damaging to the healthy development of a discipline which is in the last analysis one of the social sciences. There was a time, not so long ago, when most of us were quite happy to accept the proposition that the social and human sciences can be "value free" and independent of their cultural and social framework. It is undoubtedly true that, whatever the case may be, this has become today a highly controversial issue, and not only for social psychology. Even the outwardly neutral description above of social psychology as the "scientific study of human social behaviour" has not managed to remain *au-dessus de la mêlée*.

For all these reasons, and many others, we must create a social psychology which grows simultaneously in many places, even if in some of them growth will be based, to begin with, on a transplantation from elsewhere. The European Monographs in Social Psychology do not set out to be "European" in explicit opposition, competition or contradistinction to anything else. All of them will present work done in Europe; some will take advantage of the rich cultural and social diversity of Europe; some could have been written anywhere. No discipline, however much it may change in the future, can afford to forget its roots, and the roots of much of contemporary social psychology are in the United States. But a discipline concerned with the analysis and understanding of human social life must, in order to acquire its full significance, be tested and measured against the intellectual and social requirements of many cultures. It would be sheer conceit to write that this is what we hope to achieve with the publication of the European Monographs. What we do hope, however, is that they will contribute to the interest and creativity of a discipline which, though potentially of great importance, has not yet managed to break out of its various parochialisms.

Bristol   HENRI TAJFEL
July 1971

CONTENTS

Part I

GENERAL BACKGROUND

Introduction

E. A. CARSWELL AND R. ROMMETVEIT

The tone of the present monograph is set by a flavour of discontent with the present state of affairs in psycholinguistic research. Most of the present research in psycholinguistics was stimulated by Chomsky's publication in 1957 of "Syntactic Structures". Since its very conception, the discipline of psycholinguistics has tended to follow very closely the lead taken by linguistics, which has proved somewhat unfortunate, as the tendency among Chomskian linguists has been to consider "the communication process as an abstraction" (Moscovici, 1967, p. 226).

The resulting linguistic description is a formalized language or logistic system with all the exceptions and ungrammatical loose ends trimmed off (Dixon, 1963, p. 51). As Chomsky himself has described the approach, "Linguistic theory is concerned primarily with an ideal speaker-listener, in a completely homogeneous speech-community, who knows its language perfectly and is unaffected by such grammatically irrelevant conditions as memory limitations, distractions, shifts of attention and interest, and errors (random or characteristic) in applying his knowledge of the language in actual performance" (Chomsky, 1965, p. 3). As Moscovici expresses it: "In wanting to make language an autonomous and purely formal entity, linguistics has forgotten the speaking subject and has created a mirror image, equally formal and autonomous, of communication" (Moscovici, 1967, p. 227).

Since these linguists are concerned with constructing a logical system involving the ideal speaker-hearer, they are unconcerned with observations of what actually does occur in specific circumstances. Any theory of non- or extralinguistic settings of the speech act is dismissed, because it would have to encompass all the individual's knowledge about the sphere of communication and this would be ever changing, and therefore incomplete (Katz and Fodor, 1962; Dixon, 1963).

The study of background knowledge of communication settings might seem more appropriate in the domain of psychology. However, although

3

the psychologist's domain has tended to involve the study of individual linguistic performance as contrasted with the linguist's focus on idealized linguistic competence, the psycholinguistic movement has followed linguistic advances very closely and has more often dealt with the problem of correlating psychological processes with logical linguistic structures than with language as a communication process.

Ervin-Tripp and Slobin (1966) have described the psycholinguists' role in the study of language: "To psychologists remains the challenge of finding the processes by which the competence described by linguists is acquired by children and is reflected in performance under a variety of conditions" (p. 436). Like the linguists, psycholinguists too have tended to strip language of its communicative nature and have taken it into the laboratory where isolated aspects of the individual's mastery of the language code are investigated by means of rote learning, perceptual tests, and other experimental manipulations. "We detach words from utterance and utterances from their proper communication settings in order to gain insight into very different aspects of words and language processing. Such procedures are legitimate and even essential, provided we realize that in each case we are dealing with fragments that outside the laboratory are embedded in extremely complex patterns of message transmission. If our ultimate aim is understanding language in action, we shall therefore be on guard against potential experimental artifacts" (Rommetveit, 1967, p. 303). Chomsky himself has seen "that rote recall is a factor of minute importance in ordinary use of language" (1964, p. 8). Thus the findings of these artificial laboratory experiments certainly must be weighed carefully.

Although the pitfalls of laboratory experimental settings are very real, it is generally accepted by psychologists that it is extremely difficult to make precise observations in a totally natural setting; in order to study the *same* situation across individuals it is necessary to exercise some degree of control. As a result it is not advocated that we leave the laboratory and focus on naturalistic observations only, but that we should treat language as the communication process it is, at the same time making some attempt to explore the extralinguistic setting in a systematic fashion, and eventually trying to subject important aspects of context to experimental control and manipulation.

Recently there has been a good deal of argument on the part of both psychologists and linguists in favour of what is being advocated here, of putting language back where it belongs, in the communication setting, with emphasis being directed toward the social nature of language. There is a new commitment to attempt to transcend the established boundaries of psycholinguistics, to expand the focus of research to view language as a fragment of a more inclusive pattern of human behaviour. Also philosophers of science of the hermeneutic-dialectic school (Apel, 1968; Habermas, 1968) have been repeatedly arguing for the necessity of a grammar of the language games in which we participate in everyday communication ("eine Sprachspielgrammatik"). It is very difficult at present to visualize how such a grammar would look. Rommetveit has argued (1970), however, that Chomsky's structural analysis exhibits an expansion of scope as it proceeds from the surface toward deeper strata and verges on involving complex patterns of communication. The deep structures of the language game may possibly become more and more visible as we expand our analysis of the utterance from its abstract syntactic form, via its content, toward the patterns of communication in which it is embedded.

The need for reconsidering the aims or directions of both linguistics and psycholinguistics has been driven home with the realization that language cannot easily be studied as a code alone, without taking into account the critical role of semantics or meaning. In the early days of the modern linguistic trend, attention tended to be focused on the structure of the code alone, but now attempts are being made to incorporate meaning, as it is readily recognized that the language code is merely the vehicle for the transmission of messages or meaning. However, it is still firmly argued by many linguists and psycholinguists that as we are only at the beginning of understanding the complexities of linguistic structure and of grasping psychological correlates of these linguistic structures, research should proceed cautiously, step by step. Inquiries into subtle relationships between what is said and what is mediated by other means should therefore be postponed until we know more about the verbal medium as such. On the other hand, the present contributors might argue that this approach may itself be considered adventurous as it obscures the very nature of language; it implies that psychological aspects of words and utterances can be captured *in vacuo*, without any systematic reference to the historically, sociologically, and psychologically defined extralinguistic situation in which they are embedded. As early as 1961 Slama-Cazacu emphasized the fact that language is not a self-contained system, but that it functions within a communication setting. Reichling (1963) and Uhlenbeck have gone further to take the extreme position of stressing that language essentially is meaningless when taken out of context. "Every sentence needs to be interpreted in the light of various extralinguistic data. These data are (1) the situation in which the sentence is spoken, (2) the preceding sentences, if any, (3) the hearer's knowledge of the speaker and the topics which might be discussed with him . . ." (Uhlenbeck, 1963, p. 11). Language "functions in its setting, but as soon as a speech-utterance is observed by the linguist outside of its situational setting and as soon as the frame of reference of the speaker is not taken into account the utterance becomes for him uninterpretable, that is, it becomes ambiguous. (Uhlenbeck, 1963, 11–12)." Jakobson (1961, p. 250) sees similar dangers: "Attempts to construct a model of language without any relation either to the speaker or to the hearer and thus to hypostasize a code detached from actual communication threaten to make a scholastic fiction from language."

A direction in which linguistics might proceed is suggested by Dixon (1963) in his review of Katz and Fodor's "The Structure of Semantic Theory" (1962), and Ziff's "Semantic Analysis" (1960): Linguistics needs to focus on "language as we *observe* it to be used in every sort of way and in every type of activity . . . Such a theory must take into account the situations in which language is used, and correlate the varying types of language with distinct situation-types. It will consider the relations between speakers and their language, and between hearers and the utterances they understand, as well as between writers and readers and language: all of these relationships are subsumed in a homogeneous general theory of 'language as we see it to be', in our role of scientific observers" (Ziff, 1963, pp. 32–33).

Bateson (1968), as well as Rommetveit (1967) has stressed the complex nature of communication, not only as involving extralinguistic situational components, but as involving concomitant modes of expression, like facial expression, gestures, etc., in addition to speech itself. "Linguistic events do not float among other events like oil in water; their structure is enough alike so that they can be interrelated . . . Linguistics has made a virtue of its autonomy for a long time, deliberately isolating language from other forms of human behaviour to exploit the fact that language is the easiest part of human behaviour to describe" (p. 8).

As psychological investigations of communication settings or context would necessarily involve studies of the roles of speaker and listener, the varied nature of their interaction, their intentions, purposes, motivations, etc., Moscovici (1967), among others, has foreseen that this is an area entirely appropriate to the social psychologist. "The theoretical and experimental study of classes of speakers and listeners, their intentions and actions, the circulation of information and the function of persuading undoubtedly belong to social psychology, at least in so far as the foregoing deal with the combination and selection of linguistic signs and rules" (p. 228). As Moscovici also notes, however, psychological studies of communication settings, networks, speaker-listener interactions, intentions, in the past have not focused on linguistic behaviour; in fact "the most superficial glance confirms the existence of this non-linguistic bias, which prevails generally in social psychology" (Moscovici, 1967, p. 228). Although the transmission of messages has been studied to a large extent, the relationship between transmission and the nature and organization of linguistic behaviour has not (Moscovici, 1967.

Thus it seems that as much as linguists and psycholinguists have ignored the context or communication setting in which language processes or linguistic behaviour occurs, so has social psychology ignored the nature and function of the linguistic sign system in their studies of communication processes. The time has definitely come to attempt to bridge the gap between the disciplines purporting to deal with language behaviour and communication processes. Each discipline has valuable data to offer future combined study of linguistic behaviour in communication settings, but previous findings must be re-evaluated as the whole here is certainly not equal to the sum of its parts. "Despite these restrictions, however, a rapport between these two disciplines could be established if we were to give up envisaging language without communication and communication without language" (Moscovici, 1967).

The papers presented in this monograph, although only tentative probes and preliminary investigations by social psychologists, attempt to scratch the surface of this important field of research, the relation between language and context in which it occurs.

Some of the experiments to be reported in this monograph actually resulted from a training seminar[a] at the University of Louvain, Belgium, in the summer of 1967, organized by the European Association for Experimental Social Psychology in collaboration with the Social Science Research Council's (U.S.A.) Committee on Transnational Social Psychology. The aim of this summer programme was to provide students with intensive firsthand experience with the experimental research process in its entirety. Each of the research groups designed an experiment, and carried out the experimentation. The experimental involvement provided by this seminar was intended as a type of apprenticeship system for experimental social psychologists. It was hoped that this programme would encourage the development of a professional milieu which would support basic research in social psychology at European institutions.

The language research group headed by Professor Ragnar Rommetveit found themselves unable to choose between two different, though related

[a] The Seminar was financed largely by funds granted to the Council by the National Science Foundation (U.S.A.). The planning Committee consisted of Serge Moscovici (Chairman), Jozef M. Nuttin, Jr., and Stanley Schachter. Professor Nuttin, Professor of Social Psychology and Director of the Laboratorium voor Experimentale Sociale Psychologie at the University of Louvain, served as Dean of the Training Seminar and Jos Jaspars, Lector of Social Psychology at the University of Leiden served as Associate Dean.

topics and as a result decided to research both. The first experiment dealt with the joint contribution of linguistic and extralinguistic context in message transmission; the second experiment was concerned with the effects of a linguistic variable, word order, on impression formation and retention.

Under the pressure of time (five weeks only was allotted for the seminar), these two experiments were conducted, data collected and analysed, and preliminary reports written up. They now appear in the present monograph under the titles, "Processing of Utterances in Context" (pp. 29–56) and "Order Effects in Impression Formation" (pp. 109–125), respectively. Although only initial probes into an area common to social psychology and psycholinguistics, the results were encouraging. Additional experimentation along similar lines was discussed and plans were made for subsequent, related work by individual participants at their home institutions.

This interest in the general lines of research pursued at the 1967 Louvain seminar also resulted in plans being made for a follow-up, working seminar in Oslo in the spring of 1968. This second seminar was sponsored jointly by the Norwegian Research Council for Science and the Humanities and the European Association for Experimental Social Psychology. At this second seminar the Louvain work was discussed and final reports prepared. Also, an opportunity was provided for individual participants to present their own ongoing language research for discussion and constructive criticism.

The interest, enthusiasm, and subsequent research stimulated by these seminars bears witness to the successful realization of one of the aims of the European Association for Experimental Social Psychology, namely that of furthering the development of research activities in the field. By mutual agreement of the psycholinguistic research group it was decided that the exploratory work carried out by the group should be documented in publication. In this way other researchers would be able to take advantage of the work of the participants of the Louvain and Oslo seminars.

In agreeing to publish the work from these seminars, the contributors fully recognize that a majority of the papers included are only of the nature of progress reports, that they do not constitute a clear unity either theoretically or methodologically, and that they neither separately nor jointly offer any unequivocal or final answer to the more general question of how to deal with the complexity of language in its relation to the context in which it occurs. Also it must be remembered that the contributing experimenters are primarily social psychologists, who like others in the field have focused their attentions on individual and group interactions, but have little or no experience in relating the organization and coding of linguistic behaviour to these social communication processes.

In spite of these reservations or drawbacks, it is our hope that by virtue of their very exploratory nature, the contributions presented in this monograph may give a realistic, though unpolished view of an as yet rather loosely defined research frontier. And a major purpose of such a publication as the present one can thus be considered to be that of eliciting criticism and stimulating further thinking which may lead eventually to significant revisions in theoretical outlook, to development of novel techniques, and possibly to some consolidation of research efforts and further co-operation among researchers who share an interest in the field.

A BRIEF READER'S GUIDE

Despite the lack of theoretical unity in this monograph as a whole, some general themes and suggestive theoretical interrelationships are evident among the various contributions. These the reader should be aware of and bear in mind when beginning the monograph. Rommetveit's introductory paper (pp. 13–26), for the most part, brings the existent interrelationships into focus; it makes an attempt to relate such diverse topics as microanalysis of word perception and the more global research on intra- and extralinguistic context. Contexts, the author argues, operate as factors which arouse and determine superordinate semantic states. These semantic states, in turn, affect subordinate perceptual processes and determine which referential potentialities will be activated in any particular case. Both the immediate intralinguistic context and the particular extralinguistic frame in which a given segment of discourse is embedded affect the choice or determination of referential meaning potentialities.

The Louvain Context study (pp. 57–65) is related more specifically to how the contexts in which a message is embedded affect the level of language processing under various experimental conditions. In general the results suggest that the more removed an experimental task is from what ordinarily occurs in a naturalistic setting, the greater the dependence seems to be on the lower level expressive tools of language. Thus the authors of this work would agree with the point of view stressed in the introduction that the experimental setting in which language is studied is very relevant if not critical to the interpretation of the results.

The emphasis upon *referential potentialities* of content words as opposed to the notion of rigid connections between words and *referents*, moreover, paves the way for hypotheses concerning ways in which "referents" are *established* in the process of social interaction. Henry (pp. 77–95) tries to show how this is achieved in a subtle creative social process, how discourse (particularly, ideologically loaded) must be understood as a process of construction of social realities and imposition of these realities upon the other members of the communication process rather than as an exchange of information about externally defined referents. Pêcheux (pp. 67–75) and Henry's pleas for a novel type of content analysis which can deal appropriately with the socially defined communication situation and "the syntax of connected discourse", contain a number of suggestions concerning the ways in which the existing gap between psycholinguistic and social psychological theory of social structure and communication can be bridged. Peeters' paper (pp. 97–105) represents another attempt at expanding psycholinguistics in a social psychological direction. This particular expansion of the frontier, however, relates specifically to attribution theory.

In several of the studies (Rommetveit *et al.*, pp. 29–56; Jaspars *et al.*, pp. 109–125; Wold, pp. 127–138; Skjerve, pp. 139–142; Kvale, pp. 143–158) there is a common concern with the effects of pro-active versus retroactive processes of contextual modification. One form this issue takes is found in the discussion of linkages of presupposition *vs.* implication in the experiments using pictures as contexts for utterances. A picture preceding a verbal communication may induce a cognitive state which serves to reduce the referential possibilities of the subsequent utterance (presupposition); in contrast, there may be some circumstances in which the picture or cognitive state may itself be in need of disambiguation or explanation which is provided by the subsequent utterance (implication). Pre- versus postposition of adjectives in adjective-noun combinations, which is dealt with by Jaspars *et al.* (pp. 109–125), Wold (pp. 127–138), and Skjerve (pp. 139–142), is a similar situation. In this case the issue is one of intralinguistic contextual arrangements rather than extralinguistic relationships. A noun preceding a descriptive adjective will induce a semantic state by which only a specific appropriate subregion of the adjective's entire sphere of referential possibilities is called into action, whereas the reverse word order will leave the listener in a state of indecision with respect to which subregion of reference is appropriate until the noun is given.

The reader should bear in mind the structural resemblance between *presupposition–implication* in the studies dealing with extralinguistic contextual relationships and *preposition–postposition* in the studies dealing with intralinguistic relationships, when he turns to the general explanations underlying observed relationships between contextual arrangement and retention in the various experiments. Phenomenological aspects and some more general implications of retroactive contextual modifications are discussed by Kvale (pp. 143–158).

In addition to these problems of temporal organization and its impact upon decoding and retention, there is also a definite concern with the ways in which different fragments of a composite message are nested, irrespective of temporal order. Such nesting is in part reflected in Wold's demonstration of the noun's status as a nucleus in retrieval of noun + adjectives combinations (pp. 127–138) and is also dealt with by Henry (pp. 77–95) in his discussion of the distinction between "free" and "tied" information. The problem of nesting is thus clearly a problem concerning the structure of message organization, and, as such, partly orthogonal to temporal order. The "car", for instance, is the nucleus or "free" information in the description "An old, rugged, cheap but clean car" as well as in "A car that is old, rugged, cheap, but clean." And fragments of messages (e.g. the sequence "old, rugged, cheap but clean") may be considered "tied" whenever their interpretation depends upon other particular fragments; such fragments might be, for example, a presupposition concerning aspects of the situation in which the act of speech takes place (for instance, common focus of attention on a car in front of the speaker or the hearer) or information conveyed by preceding or subsequent speech. The general problem of nesting is hence apparently at the very core of both intra- and extralinguistic context. The search for patterns of interdependence among message elements across the boundary between *what is said* and *what is seen* is hence an illustration of an expansion of structural analysis from intralinguistic form to complex patterns of communication.

REFERENCES

Apel, K. A. (1968). Die erkenntnisanthropologische Funktion der Kommunikationsgemeinschaft und die Grundlagen der Hermeneutik. *In*: "Information und Kommunikation" (Simon Hoser, ed). R. Oldenbourg, München-Wien.
Bateson, Mary Catherine (1968). Linguistics in the semiotic frame, *Linguistics* **39**, 5–17.
Chomsky, N. (1957). "Syntactic Structures," Mouton, The Hague.
Chomsky, N. (1964). "Current Issues in Linguistic Theory," Mouton, The Hague.
Chomsky, N. (1965). "Aspects of a Theory of Syntax," M.I.T. Press, Cambridge, Mass.
Dixon, R. M. W. (1963). A trend in semantics, *Linguistics* **1**, 30–57.
Dixon, R. M. W. (1964). A trend in semantics: rejoinder, *Linguistics* **4**, 14–18.
Ervin-Tripp, Susan M. and Slobin, D. I. (1966). Psycholinguistics, *Ann. Rev. Psychol.* **17**, 435–474.

Habermas, F. (1968). "Erkenntnis und Interesse," Suhrkamp Verlag, Frankfurt am Rhein.

Jakobson, R., ed. (1961). Linguistics and communication theory. *In* Structure of language and its mathematical aspects. *Amer. Math. Soc.*, 245–252.

Katz, J. J. and Fodor, J. A. (1962). "The Structure of Semantic Theory," M.I.T. Press, Cambridge, Mass.

Moscovici, S. (1967). Communication processes and the properties of language. *In*: "Advances in Experimental Social Psychology" (Berkowitz, L., ed.), Vol. 3, pp. 225–270.

Reichling, A. (1963). "Das Problem der Bedeutung in der Sprachwissenschaft," Innsbrucker Beiträge zur Kulturwissenschaft, Sonderheft 19. Innsbruck.

Rommetveit, R. (1967). "Words, Meanings, and Messages," Academic Press, New York.

Rommetveit, R. (1970). Language games, deep syntactic structures, and hermeneutic circles. Paper read at Conference on Metatheory in Social Sciences in Elsenor, Denmark, April, pp. 12–15.

Slama-Cazacu, T. (1961). "Language and context." Mouton, The Hague.

Uhlenbeck, E. M. (1963). An appraisal of transformation theory, *Lingua* 12, 1–18.

Ziff, P. (1960). "Semantic Analysis," Cornell University Press, Ithaca, N.Y.

Words, contexts, and verbal message transmission[a]

RAGNAR ROMMETVEIT

Modern psycholinguistics is a very heterogeneous and rapidly expanding field of research, and psycholinguists who are currently engaged in psycholinguistic studies came there from very different theroretical backgrounds. They have very little in common, therefore, apart from a research interest in those very aspects of language which Ebbinghaus struggled to get rid of when he first introduced linguistic stimuli into the laboratories of a young scientific psychology. Ebbinghaus' nonsense syllables and Shakespeare's words were in certain significant respects considered as belonging to entirely different domains. Only recently have experimental psychologists ventured to expand their inquiries into the latter sphere of words, meaning, and verbal message transmission.

The riddles of human language are manifold and subtle, however, and current psycholinguistic research resembles a guerrilla warfare in a vast and largely unknown territory. Experimental psychologists detach words from utterances and utterances from their proper communication settings in order to gain knowledge concerning different aspects of language processing. Some of us do experiments on speech discrimination, some are engaged in measurement of so-called affective word meaning, others employ psychological research methods to investigate semantic relationships, still others use word association tasks in order to map associative networks, and quite a few psychologists have joined structural linguists in a search for so-called surface and deep sentence structures. As a consequence, we are left with very scattered, very fragmentary and very tentative insights only, and with a challenge to bring such fragments of exploratory knowledge together into a coherent psychological picture of human language in action.

The present paper is, in a way, a response to such a challenge. We shall not even try to survey the various "schools" of psycholinguistics,

[a] Expanded version of paper presented at the psycholinguistic seminar in Oslo, May 1968.

let alone try to reconcile them into an eclectic psycholinguistic theory. Some rather important clues to the riddles of human language, however, may possibly be discovered in psychological studies of words. Words are tools for message transmission in a shared human world of objects and events. We shall try to examine them as they emerge in acts of decoding and encoding, and we shall explore sensori-perceptual processes as well as higher-order cognitive aspects of such acts. After a psychological microanalysis of the word in isolation, we shall briefly explore what happens when it appears in its natural habitat, i.e. when it constitutes an integral part of an utterance embedded in a context of human communication.

THE WORD AS A HIERARCHICALLY ORGANIZED PSYCHOLOGICAL PROCESS

Consider, first, a person from an entirely different community listening to your own language. Such a person who doesn't know any English at all might be asked to parse the preceding spoken utterance into "words" or word-like segments. He will, in all likelihood, end up with an incorrect segmentation: the whole sequence "to-your-own" might be judged to be one word only, whereas "listening" might be conceived of as two separate words (*"liste"* and "ning"). Failures like these show that purely acoustic-articulatory features of speech such as pause and intonation are insufficient cues for appropriate perceptual organization of speech. A listener who masters the language, however, has apparently additional internally provided resources at his disposal. Segments of speech acquire the status of words by a process of "active hearing": temporal strings of speech sounds are chunked in accordance with morphological and semantic rules of the language.

It seems safe to conclude, therefore, that words emerge in acts of decoding if and only if appropriate cognitive-perceptual operations are performed upon temporal strings of speech sounds or, in the case of written speech, upon particular visual forms. These cognitive-perceptual operations must somehow involve a process of recognition, i.e. a checking of the acoustic or visual stimulus input against an acquired vocabulary. Recognition of perceptual form, however, does not necessarily imply comprehension of meaning. Sometimes, I may recognize a pattern of speech sounds as an empty perceptual form only, as "a word I have heard before, but do not understand". And in the case of homonyms, perceptual forms that convey two or more very different word meanings, recognition of phonetic or visual form alone leaves me in a state of indecision.

Let us consider for a moment the sequence of letters STRENG, the common mediator of two very different Norwegian words. When it is used as a stimulus in a word association list and preceded by nouns referring to cords, ribbons, etc., it generates a noun meaning "string". In a word association list of Norwegian adjectives for personal attributes, on the other hand, it is usually experienced as an adjective corresponding to the English word "severe". Entirely different word association responses to the very same letter sequence in the two different settings provide evidence that different words emerged in decoding of the same visual stimulus input (Rommetveit and Strømnes, 1965). A spontaneous choice among different semantic alternatives is also required whenever we encounter words with multiple but related meanings, such as the English words "play" and "board".

Recognition and choice are not unique to speech perception. Some more subtle and possibly unique aspects of the word, however, may perhaps be brought to our attention when particular tricks are played upon linguistic stimulus input in the laboratory. In one series of experiments, a stereo-tachistoscope was used to introduce binocular rivalry of letters (Rommetveit, Berkley and Brøgger, 1968; Rommetveit and Kleiven, 1968). Short strings of typewritten or typed letters were exposed for periods of 170 or 200 msec, and subjects were asked to report as accurately as possible what they saw. The stereograms contained strings of letters such as *sog/sor* and *sug/sur*, and the letters *g* and *r* would then compete for the same position in the subject's visual field.

What was seen under such conditions of brief exposure and binocular rivalry was, to a large extent, determined by purely linguistic properties of the two monocular images and their possible combinations. This was the case with the two rivals *g* and *r*. They were seen as *g* only, as *r* only, as *gr* and as *rg*, depending upon which resolution of the rivalry conflict yielded a word. *Sug/sur* was thus seen by nearly everybody as either the Norwegian word "sug" or the Norwegian word "sur", and most subjects were highly confident that there were only those three letters "out there". *Sog/sor*, on the other hand, was by many subjects clearly seen as *sorg*. Whether both or only one of the two competing letters were seen, was thus obviously not a matter of rivalling visual forms only. The experience of the word "sorg" in response to the two non-word images *sog* and *sor* testifies to a process of word formation in which the perceiver intuitively betrays his mastery of morphological rules.

These and a number of other experimental studies provide us with a psychological picture of the word as a very complex and hierarchically organized *process*. Sequences of speech sounds and written strings of letters are as such devoid of meaning, but words emerge in acts of decoding when such stimuli are met with an internally provided request for some meaningful message element. The process by which words emerge out of acoustic or visual stimulus input may therefore be schematically visualized as a complex test-operate-test-exit mechanism (a TOTE mechanism, see Miller *et al.*, 1960). When the input (I) is tested against a request for some appropriate message element (T_x), a state of incongruity will necessarily arise (see Fig. 1). Hence, a very complex operate (O_x) is initiated, the final outcome of which is again tested against the superordinate request for meaning. Congruity between test and outcome will lead to exit (E), i.e. to the execution of the entire programme for message reception for that particular input. This means simply that comprehension has taken place, and that the TOTE mechanism is available for novel stimulus input.

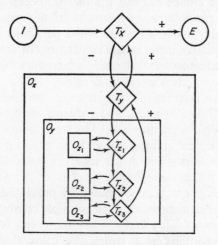

FIG. 1. A TOTE hierarchical model for generation of words from strings of letters: (I) input, (O) operate, (T) test, (E) exit, and ($+$, $-$) outcome of test. O_{z1-3}: generation of word form: T_{z1-3}: test for word form; O_y: search for semantic correlate (s); O_x: choice of specific semantic correlate; and T_x: test for specific semantic correlate as part of message.

The operate (O_x), however, must be conceived of as some sort of a Chinese box, with subordinate TOTE units embedded in it. The test at the immediately subordinate level may be thought of as a matching of an already identified *word form* against admissible semantic correlates or "meanings". A negative outcome at this level yields the experience of "a word I have heard before, but do not understand". Tests at the lowest level (T_z), finally, involve a matching of stimulus input against familiar perceptual forms.

The *operations* required at this lowest level (O_z) under conditions of tachistoscopic word recognition are, in very simple cases, a position-by-position reading of letters from left to right (O_{z1}). This is prohibited under conditions of binocular rivalry of letters, however, since there are two different letters occupying one and the same position in the visual field. Therefore, a second operation (O_{z2}) is initiated, by which first one and then the other of the two competing letters is simply ignored. This operation yields a positive outcome when both images are word strings of letters such as *sug/sur*. It fails for non-word images such as *sog/sor*, however, and a third operation (O_{z3}) is then required. The two rivals are then both registered and rearranged in space, first in one order and then in the opposite. *R* and *g*, for instance, occur always in the order *rg* in endings, whereas they can only appear as *gr* in beginnings of Norwegian words. And this is exactly what happens to them when they are rivals in stereograms such as *sog/sor* and *gøt/røt*: the former is seen as *sorg*, the latter as *grøt*.

The main lesson to be learned from these experiments on binocular rivalry of letters, perhaps, is a suspicion that words can only be explored psychologically as very complex *processes*, that subordinate perceptual operations are embedded as "sub-routines" in higher-order mental operations, and that entirely novel perceptual tactics may develop when such tactics are required in order for a perceiver to generate meaning. The perceived word is thus as much a product of efferent processes as of afferent processes, and strictly analogous considerations can be brought to bear upon the spoken word. *Homonymy* is thus most appropriately described as a purely incidental convergence of entirely different higher-order processes. It so happens that Norwegians have to produce the same sound pattern ("streng") when talking about severity and strings, i.e. the same sensori-motoric "subroutines" serve entirely different higher-order purposes of message transmission.

The hierarchical structure of the word may also be explored in terms of which part processes are "attended to" and "accessible to awareness". In general, we would expect residuals of lower level operations to fade away once they have provided appropriate input for higher levels; we attend to the message conveyed by linguistic stimuli rather than to the perceptual tactics by which messages are generated. The dominance of *meaning* over *perceptual form* is experienced as a serious obstacle by the proof reader. A content-orientated reader experiences a dilemma; his duty is to check for typographical errors and deviations from appropriate perceptual forms, but his interest is geared toward meaning. His dilemma seems to arise from a lack of capacity to attend to more than one level of the hierarchy at a time. Typographical errors tend to go unnoticed if he attends to meaning, whereas a careful attention to perceptual form prohibits comprehension of meaning.

A somewhat similar state of incompatibility may possibly occur under conditions of semantic satiation of words. Continued fixation of a written word form or repeated exposure to a spoken word form allow for a prolonged period of low level processing, far beyond the very minimal time required in order for semantic attribution to occur. Once the subordinate operations have served to "excess" their function of providing input to the highest level, we may expect a detachment to occur. Mere repetition of them as autonomous perceptual activities may then attract the attention that ordinarily is focused upon the highest level only. This shift of attention from higher to lower levels of the hierarchy may possibly account for the experienced "loss of meaning" and the concomitant strange experience of empty perceptual form.

The perceptual forms (whether acoustic or graphic) under ordinary conditions of verbal communication thus have apparently hardly any function other than that of providing appropriate input to higher-order semantic and cognitive processes. We comprehend, and may even remember, ideas and messages, but we do not ordinarily store the acoustic or visual images by which ideas and messages were conveyed. This has also been experimentally confirmed in a study by Kolers (1965). Kolers had French-English bilinguals learn mixed lists of French and English words. The clearly subordinate status of perceptual form was then reflected in recall, in the high frequency with which a French word was given back in terms of its English equivalent and vice versa. What appears to be attended to, accessible in immediate memory and stored even in word recall tasks, thus is the highest level apparently, that of semantic attribution.

SEMANTIC ATTRIBUTION AND ASSESSMENT
OF WORD MEANING POTENTIALITIES

What, then, have psycholinguists to say about semantic attribution and word meaning? First of all, perhaps, some words of caution concerning search for word meanings. Words differ markedly with respect to their functions in message transmission. Some words have hardly any independent functions at all, but may nevertheless contribute to message transmission when they appear in particular linguistic contexts. The definite article, for example, may be said to have a dependent semantic value (Reichling, 1963), although it conveys nothing in itself. When I am visiting a friend, however, and he says: "The dog has disappeared", I most likely assume that *his* dog has been lost. What is achieved, therefore, is what Reichling has labelled "eine Als-bekannt-Setzung". Other words serve purely *deictic* or *pointing* functions. Demonstrative pronouns such as "*this*" and "*that*" refer to whatever the speaker and the listener temporarily attend to or have in mind, be it a delicious dish of food or a very sophisticated psychological theory. Psychological studies of word meaning, however, have dealt almost exclusively with words that are said to have some autonomous, inherent signification, with so-called content words or designators such as "silly", "beautiful", "rat", "poison", "beg", "capitalism" and "vacation". And let us now see how the meaning of such content words may be assessed in terms of psychological processes

We have to assume, first of all, an initial *process of reference* (R_1). Somehow, the word *form* must activate conceptual or representational processes. In the case of homonyms, distinctively different processes of reference are involved. If STRENG triggers a reference to a particular kind of cord, we shall expect one pattern of subsequent associative processes; if it triggers a process of reference to some personal attribute, on the other hand, we expect entirely different associations and concomitant affective processes. An initial process of reference is thus a prerequisite for subsequent associative and potential affective part processes.

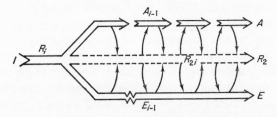

FIG. 2. The word as a three-component temporal pattern: I: Input (word form); R_1: act of reference, choice of specific semantic correlate; R_2: process of representation (sustained); A: associative process; and E: emotive process.

Somehow, however, some process of representation (R_2) must be sustained over time beyond the stage of initiating associations and affective processes, and the sustained representation is then very likely affected by concomitant associations (A) and emotive processes (E). Consider, for instance, the processes triggered by the word form "*horse*" in two situations in which I have nothing else to do than to ponder its meaning. On one occasion, it may remind me of one particular horse, the delight I experienced when riding that horse, etc. On the other occasion, residuals of my zoological school training may dominate my associative chain. The initial process of reference is assumed to be the same in the two cases. A magic cross-cut into subsequent processes (R_2, A and E), however, would probably reveal somewhat different "horses". The sustained representation is most likely enriched by somewhat different concomitant associative and emotive processes on the two occasions.

What we propose is thus a very crude and schematic three-component model of word meaning: an initial process of reference is assumed to branch off into sustained representation, affecting and affected by an associative and an affective activity. The relative contributions of the assumed three components, however, may vary from one communication setting to the other. Consider the word "*democracy*" in the following three contexts:

1. I am listening to a lecture on modern history, and the lecturer says: "Democracy, however, presupposes very specific economic and educational conditions".

2. I am listening to an actor reading a poem: "Democracy . . . (long pause), "battles were fought for ideas . . .".

3. I am listening to a speech on our National Independence Day: ". . . and as good Norwegians, we shall always remain devoted to democracy!"

It seems reasonable to assume that conceptual–representational processes (R_2) are a fairly dominant component of the entire meaning pattern in the lecture context whereas associative processes (A) are relatively more dominant in the context of the poem, and that purely emotive processes (E) constitute a very significant component when the word appears in the patriotic speech. It seems reasonable to expect, moreover, that abstract representational-conceptual processes become an increasingly salient and dominant component of word meaning with age, as the child's general intellectual capacity develops. The predominance of the emotive component in younger children has been demonstrated in word sorting tasks. Rommetveit and Hundeide (1967) asked children at different age levels to sort sets of familiar words. Each set had been selected so that it fitted into a fourfold table: they were either "good" or "bad" words, and half of all good and bad words referred to one class of objects whereas the other half referred to a different class. Thus, one set contained the Norwegian words for hospital, squirrel, cottage, wolf, crocodile, castle, rat, villa, hovel, butterfly, pussycat, and prison. With the latter two words ("pussycat", a *good animal*, and "prison", a *bad building*) given as cue words, the set could now be split into two halves in two different ways. The child either sorts out as similar to "pussycat" all *good* words, irrespective of reference ("squirrel", "cottage", "castle", "villa" and "butterfly"), or he could pick all *animal* words irrespective of their emotive loadings ("squirrel", "wolf", "crocodile", "rat", "butterfly").

Young children adopted a purely emotive strategy of sorting (good versus bad words) significantly more frequently than older ones. In addition, a correspondence was revealed between word sorting and subsequent recall. Again, a diagonal pair (like "pussycat" and "prison") were provided as cues, and the child was asked to try to reproduce the entire list. Emotive sorters then introduced significantly more novel words which were emotively in agreement with the cue word only (i.e. "candy" being introduced below "pussycat"). Children who had sorted on the basis of reference, on the other hand, introduced more novel words resembling the cue word with respect to reference only (i.e. "snake" being reproduced below "pussycat").

In addition to situational and developmental factors determining word meaning patterns, we encounter considerable differences between different sets of content words. Some words, such as *"nigger"* in the American language, have a very significant and well-defined emotive function. In addition to its reference, the word "nigger" conveys a hostile attitude toward coloured people. Other words, such as "democracy", "crime" and "communism", appear to have ambiguous and dual functions of reference and signalling of affect. Still others, such as "rectilinear", "vertical", and "transform", are nearly devoid of emotive loading. The interrelationships between the various assumed part processes of word meaning appear to be very subtle, however, and have hardly been systematically investigated at all.

THE ASSESSMENT OF MEANING POTENTIALITIES OF THE ISOLATED WORD AND THE ACTIVATION OF SUCH POTENTIALITIES IN PARTICULAR CONTEXTS

Our tentative evidence concerning components of word meaning stems mainly from studies of the isolated word in the psychological laboratory. Such settings allow us to inquire into meaning *potentialities*, but very little has been said so far about the ways in which such potentialities are brought into action in natural contexts of verbal communication.

When the word occurs in an utterance, there is first of all a drastic reduction of the time available for its processing. For example, consider the following excerpt from a discourse:

"The distance from the last cottage on your right to the intersection where you take a left turn is approximately two miles. From that intersection you can see a red barn . . ." If I pursued associative pathways of "cottage" into remote parts of its associative networks while listening to such an utterance, I would probably be entirely lost in associative thought at the moment the speaker has come to "a left turn". Even lakes and fishing and mountains that constitute very central elements of its associative network are probably left out when the word "cottage" appears in such an utterance. The most obvious effect of context is thus

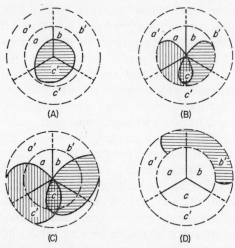

(A)   (B)

(C)   (D)

FIG. 3. Different patterns of activation of word meaning potentialities. Sectors *a*, *b* and *c* represent major features of the core meaning, whereas *a'*, *b'*, and *c'* represent fringe features connected to those areas. Shaded regions represent meaning components operant in the actual setting. (A) instances 1–4, (B) instances 5*a*–8*b*, (C) instances 9*a* and 9*b*, and (D) instances 10*a* and 10*b*.

a process of elimination (see Fig. 3, A); only a fraction of those meaning potentialities which are assessed by requests for definition, word association tasks, and semantic differential measurements appears to be operant in any particular context. A skeleton of a process of reference only, and no associative fringe or emotive meaning, is required in response to "cottage" in the utterance conveying driving instructions. The initial process of reference, however, appears to be a *sine qua non* for comprehension of the message, and hence it may be said to constitute the "core meaning" of content words.

An elimination of associative fringe and secondary affective processes, however, is by no means the whole story. A careful examination of the dictionary will convince us that almost every word has a whole sphere of referential and related associative possibilities. The "water" I encounter in a poem about a thirsty and nostalgic Norwegian sailor in Hong Kong is thus distinctively different from the "water" in the chemistry book. In the context of the poem, "drinkability" will very likely be a dominant feature of reference, and the associative fringe may be one of "glasses" and "beverage". In the other context, fragments of chemical knowledge will probably enter the sustained representation.

Like most other words, "water" seems to encompass an abundance of referential-associative-emotive potentialities. Both drinkability and chemical formulae may thus appear in my response to the word in a word-association task, when I have ample time to ponder its meaning via multiple strategies of reference and related associative pathways. In a particular linguistic context, however, there is very often a pro-active constraint upon processing; only very selected features of reference and association will fit the frame provided by what has already been said.

What is brought into action then sometimes is only a particular part of "the core meaning" such as the feature "*maleness*" or "*adulthood*" of the word "man" (see Fig. 3, B), for instance. This will be the case when the word appears in questions such as:

"Who opened the door, a woman or a man?"

"Who opened the door, a boy or a man?"

In other cases, entirely different potentialities such as an associative fringe of masculinity and courage are brought into action. This is probably what happens when I read the following about a soldier: "He had really shown that he was a man" (Fig. 3, D). Information concerning humanness, adulthood and maleness in the latter case has been amply provided by the preceding text, and the word form is thus free to convey fringe meaning related to, e.g., the maleness feature. A contextually induced semantic state will thus, in all cases, interfere at the superordinate level of the word process, and in such a way that only particular, contextually appropriate parts of the entire pattern of meaning potentialities are activated.

In other cases, some retroactive process is obviously required. When polysemous word forms appear as initial elements of utterances, for instance, decoding must be postponed. Consider the following examples:

"The ball I went to buy yesterday was expensive".

"The ball I went to yesterday was boring."

The inherent ambiguity of "ball" cannot be resolved immediately. The word form is hence probably processed only at a lower level and kept in storage until subsequent information allows for an unequivocal semantic attribution. In still other cases, an initial process of reference may be retroactively *enriched* by particular associative and emotive fringe processes. Consider, again, an example:

"Only a man and two women were at the station."

"Only a man would be able to endure the hardships of the coal mine." Identical processes should be triggered by "man" at the moment the words "Only a man" and nothing more has been heard. Any additional features (e.g. of masculinity) which differentiate the man in the coal mine from the man at the station, therefore, must derive from a retroactive process.

Speech comprehension then may be analysed as semantic decision-making along the temporal axis of the utterance and some of the decisions have to do with deciding which of a variety of meaning potentialities were encoded in a given form. Disambiguation, i.e., selection of a particular and contextually appropriate subregion of the area of meaning potentialities in Fig. 3, is sometimes instantaneous. Extralinguistic context or preceding speech has then induced a superordinate semantic state (T_x in Fig. 1) which controls the cognitive output of the word process at the moment of perception. For instance, consider the word "craft" and its entire domain of referential possibilities (Weinrich, 1966, p. 430). On one occasion, I am sitting with a friend on a shore watching the boats passing by, and my friend says: "*Which craft would you prefer?*" The meaning of "craft" is then immediately restricted to "watercraft" (e.g. the horizontally shaded subregion in Fig. 3B). Precisely the same selective activation is achieved when I encounter the word in a linguistic context such as "*I should like to sail a craft some day*".

When clarification is achieved retroactively, on the other hand, the hearer is sometimes temporarily left in a state of uncertainty equal to the entire domain of meaning potentialities. Final semantic attribution must then be postponed until some subsequent linguistic or extra-linguistic input allows the hearer to decide which subregion of potentialities has been encoded. In the meantime, the semantically ambiguous element must be kept in storage in immediate memory in some form. Some of the reports to follow (Jaspars *et al.*, pp. 109–125; Kvale, pp. 143–158; Wold, pp. 127–138) deal with the impact of such retroactive mechanisms of decoding upon storage and retrieval.

The notion of a sphere of referential and associative potentialities allows for systematic investigations of the impact of extralinguistic and intralinguistic contexts upon reference. What constitutes so-called "free" (i.e. assumed) information in a given discourse, for instance, may often be determined by a tacit contract between participants, by virtue of convergence of assumptions and/or their loci within a social structure. The referent of "water" in the context of the textbook of chemistry is thus obviously determined by the institutional frame of scientific education in which it is embedded. Such social determinants of referents of messages will be explored by Paul Henry (pp. 77–95).

The discreteness and strict temporal segmentation of speech thus are clearly at variance with the processing of word meaning when words are embedded in spoken utterances. The articulatory-acoustic channel of speech sound transmission does not allow for more than one sound to get across at any given time. This universal and severe constraint upon human languages, however, is very efficiently counteracted. Long strings of speech are chunked into segments such as word forms, and identical perceptual forms mediate different meaning potentialities in different communication settings. Psychological studies of words *qua* complex cognitive-perceptual-motor processes may therefore be said to provide us with some tentative, yet very important clues to some of the riddles of human languages. They may help us understand how an infinite variety of messages can be transmitted by temporal chains of a very limited number of speech sounds.

REFERENCES

Henry, P. (1971). On processing of message referents in contexts. *In* "Social Contexts of Messages" (E. A. Carswell and R. Rommetveit, eds), pp. 77–95. Academic Press, London and New York.

Jaspars, J., Rommetveit, R., Cook, M., Havelka, N., Henry, P., Herkner, W., Pêcheux, M. and Peeters, G. (1971). Order effects in impression formation. *In* "Social Contexts of Messages" (E. A. Carswell and R. Rommetveit, eds), pp. 109–125. Academic Press, London and New York.

Kolers, P. (1965). Bilingual facilitation of short term memory words remembered with respect to semantic rather than morphemic properties. Paper presented at the Eastern Psychological Association meeting in Atlantic City, New Jersey.

Kvale, S. The temporal perspective of remembering. *In* "Social Contexts of Messages" (E. A. Carswell and R. Rommetveit, eds), pp. 143–158. Academic Press, London and New York.

Miller, G. A., Galanter, E. and Pribram, K. H. (1960). "Plans and the Structure of Behavior," Holt, Rinehart and Winston, New York.

Reichling, A. (1963). Das Problem der Bedeutung in der Sprachwissenschaft. Innsbrucker Beiträge zur Kulturwissenschaft, Sonderheft 19. Innsbruck.

Rommetveit, R. (1968). "Words, Meanings and Messages: Theory and Experiments in Psycholinguistics," Academic Press and Universitetsforlaget, New York, London and Oslo.

Rommetveit, R., Berkley, M. and Brøgger, J. (1968). Generation of words from stereoscopically presented non-word strings of letters, *Scandinavian Journal of Psychology* **9**, 150–156.

Rommetveit, R. and Hundeide, V. (1967). Emotive and representational components of meaning in word sorting and recall, *Pedagogisk Forskning* **11**, 47–59.

Rommetveit, R. and Kleiven, J. (1968). Word generation, A replication. *Scand. J. Psychol.* **9**, 277–281.

Rommetveit, R. and Strømnes, F. (1965). Determinants of interpretation of homonyms in a word association context, *Pedagogisk Forskning* **9**, 179–184.

Weinreich, U. (1966). Explorations in semantic theory. *In* "Current Trends in Linguistics. Theoretical Foundations" (T. A. Sebeok, ed.), Vol. 3, pp. 395–477. Mouton, The Hague.

Wold, A. H. (1971). Impression formation. A psycholinguistic approach. *In* "Social Contexts of Messages" (E. A. Carswell and R. Rommetveit, eds), pp. 127–138. Academic Press, London and New York.

Part II

THE UTTERANCE IN ITS EXTRALINGUISTIC AND SOCIAL CONTEXT

Processing of Utterances in Context

RAGNAR ROMMETVEIT, MALCOLM COOK, NENAD
HAVELKA, PAUL HENRY, WERNER HERKNER,
MICHEL PÊCHEUX and GUIDO PEETERS[a]

Some recently developed models of language processing are derived from experiments on learning, overlearning, and reproduction of lists of entirely unrelated sentences. Syntactic structure has been the main focus of inquiry in these cases and a number of the investigations have dealt with structural complexity as assessed by Chomsky's early analysis of syntactic transformations (Chomsky, 1957). Thus experiments by Mehler and Miller (1964) and Savin and Perchonock (1965) have been said to support the hypotheses that the utterance is recoded into semantic content and syntactic form: a complex sentence appears to be decoded and stored in memory in terms of its simplest (kernel) form plus "syntactic footnotes".

Johnson (1965) had subjects learn lists of sentences according to a paired associate paradigm, each sentence being preceded by a particular digit. Recall performance then was matched against a strictly left-to-right proceeding reproduction of the sentence in response to that digit and was measured in terms of transitional errors between contiguous words. Errors were most frequent between words belonging to different major syntactic constituents (such as *noun phrase* and *verb phrase*), whereas few errors were observed at the transitions between words belonging to the same phrase. The syntactic organization of the utterance may hence be said to affect its processing; in decoding, storage and retrieval, associations appear to be formed between "encoding steps" (or "nodes" in the phrase structure) rather than between contiguous words.

These laboratory conditions for language processing differ, however, in a number of ways from most natural settings of verbal message transmission. Outside the laboratory utterances are usually embedded in more inclusive communication processes. Some appropriate context is provided for the utterance by preceding speech, nonlinguistic aspects

[a] Working paper of the European Research Training Seminar in Experimental Social Psychology, University of Louvain, 1967.

of the situation, or by preceding speech and nonlinguistic aspects jointly. Comprehension and retrieval of the message, moreover, is revealed most often in behaviours other than exact reproduction of the words by which the message was conveyed. And, finally, repeated exposure to an utterance is hardly the normal case in a communication situation unless the listener has some difficulty in hearing or understanding what is being said, or except in particular cases when there is a request, not only for appropriate message transmission, but for verbatim recall of linguistic form. What appears outside the laboratory to be a subordinate tool of message transmission may hence, in the sentence learning experiment, be attended to in its own right. Absence of appropriate contexts, repetition, and a request for reproduction of an utterance are likely to induce a particular medium-bound set (Rommetveit, 1968, p. 209).

The evidence for "syntactic footnotes" in sentence recall thus stems from retrieval performance at a stage when the subject has learned, and even overlearned, the content of the utterance (Mehler and Miller, 1964). His problem then is no longer to retrieve *what* was said, but *how* it was said. What is assessed by Johnson's measure of transitional errors, moreover, is clearly failures of strictly sequential verbatim reproduction rather than deficient message retrieval. Consider, for instance, the stimulus sentence "*The tall boy saved the dying woman*" (Johnson, 1965) and the following hypothetical retrieval performances:

(a) "The tall boy came . . ."
(b) "The boy helped a woman."
(c) "The big boy did a brave deed."
(d) "A dying woman was saved by the tall boy."

Any reasonable measure of message retrieval would yield a ranking of performances such that (d) is superior to (a). More or less appropriate re-encodings of message elements, such as those appearing in (b) through (d), are simply dealt with as errors when transitional error probabilities are assessed. Order of achievement, according to Johnson's analysis, must be determined strictly by *the location of the first-appearing error of reproduction* and hence be (a) > (b) = (c) > (d).

Tannenbaum and Williams (1966), using Johnson's method of paired associate learning, studied reproduction of ordinary as well as "meaningless" (semantically anomalous) sentences. The latter were harder to learn. Once they were learned, however, they were reproduced with fewer transitional errors than was the case with meaningful sentences. Word order appears therefore to play a particularly important role in learning and retention of utterances that fail to convey any immediately comprehensible message.

Models of language processing based upon sentence learning experiments such as those by Johnson (1965) and Mehler and Miller (1964) may be said to apply to the utterance in a rote learning situation rather than ordinary conditions of verbal message transmission. The particular words and specific syntactic structure of the utterance are essential in the initial decoding. However, what is being stored and retrieved under ordinary conditions of message transmission most likely are neither words nor "syntactic footnotes", but higher-order message elements. Retrieval therefore implies *re-encoding*. Whether re-encoding will yield an exact reproduction of the utterance by which the message was conveyed in the first place, then, will depend upon a number of factors. One very important factor will be the availability of equivalent linguistic tools such as synonymous words, options of word orders, and functionally equivalent sentence frames. Thus what appears to be retention of specific linguistic forms upon a closer examination may be more appropriately understood as cases of a perfect match between decoding and encoding processes. This possibility has been brought to the foreground in a study by Kolers (1965) in which French-English bilinguals were asked to memorize and reproduce a mixed list of French and English words. Evidence for re-encoding under these conditions was established by the high frequency with which a stimulus word presented in one language was retrieved in the other. The apparent "verbatim recall" by unilingual subjects memorizing lists of words may hence be due to a one-to-one relationship between concepts and word forms and thus, in some important respects, incidental.

Concepts such as "re-encoding", "higher-order message element", and "linguistic tool" presuppose a hierarchical relationship between a message and the utterance by which it is transmitted. Consider the utterance *"It's a shame she did not get there in time"*. The initial part of the utterance ("It's a shame . . .") may be said to convey *regret* on the part of the speaker, and this higher-order message element may under a variety of conditions be equally well transmitted by other linguistic tools such as *"It's a pity . . ."*, *"It's regrettable . . ."*, and *"It's unfortunate"*. It may even be conveyed by non-linguistic means such as concomitant expressive behaviours. For example, the speaker may convey regret by a facial expression as he says: *"She did not get there in time"*. And the message conveyed by the entire utterance (regret concerning late arrival) may be nearly perfectly re-encoded in a different utterance such as *"It's a pity she was too late"*.

Such re-encoding is likely to occur often when messages are transmitted and retrieved in everyday life. Consider the following case. Two men are standing at a railway station, both of them being worried about a lady they know who is supposed to catch the next train. As the train leaves the station, one of them says: "*It's a shame she did not get there in time*". The other man departs to join his wife, who asks: "What did he say?", and her husband answers: "*He said it's a pity she was too late*". Next consider retrieval of the very same sentence when the digit stimulus cue for it appears for the nth time on the memory drum in a learning experiment. In these two cases processing appears to proceed at *different levels*. The output of decoding and input of encoding in the former case are clearly higher-order message elements. On the other hand, what is being learned, stored and retrieved in the memory drum task, are particular linguistic tools.

The intuitively felt difference between the rote learning situation and the particular "natural" communication setting described above, however, may possibly be broken down into more specific components. The extra effect of mere repetition in the learning experiment can be eliminated by focusing upon the first retrieval only. The impact of an appropriate context, moreover, may be explored in the laboratory. For instance, a drawing of a train leaving a station may be presented immediately before the utterance instead of a digit.

The purpose of the present study will be to investigate recall of utterances under experimental conditions which more closely resemble everyday situations of verbal message transmission than do the sentence learning experiments briefly discussed above. The focus will be upon variables which are hypothesized to affect efficiency of message transmission and level of processing; more specifically, the emphasis will be upon the ways in which particular contexts of utterances affect message transmission under different conditions of retrieval.

An attempt will be made to explore some relationships between an utterance as a whole and some immediately preceding stimulus event. The latter will be a *non-appropriate context* if its relationship to the utterance is one of sheer temporal proximity only. This will be the case, for instance, when some arbitrarily chosen geometrical figure is introduced as a ready signal for the spoken utterance: "*It's a shame she did not get there in time*". *Appropriate contexts*, on the other hand, should resemble events prompting verbal message transmission in natural communication settings. This will be the case if, instead of the geometrical figure, a drawing of a train leaving a station appears as a ready signal for the utterance given above.

The departing train sets the stage for a message concerning late arrival and should hence facilitate decoding, storing, and retrieval of higher-order message elements. The relationship in this case is unidirectional and may be said to be one of *presupposition*. In other cases, a bi-directional relationship of *presupposition and implication* (Ducrot, 1966) seems to exist between context and utterance.

The terms "implication" and "presupposition" can be further illuminated by considering all possible combinations of truth values for an ordered pair of atomic propositions, p and q. The statement "p implies q" excludes only the possibility that q is true and p is false. Consider now the ordered pair of a given picture context and an utterance as fitting into such a scheme, i.e. that their connection is essentially one of logical implication. A given interpretation of the utterance (second element of ordered pair) will then exclude a whole range of interpretations of the picture (first element). The hearer may just have been watching a fading flower, for instance, when he is told: "*There was insufficient light and heat*". The sight of the flower will then most likely prepare the stage for the subsequent message. The latter, however, serves to *explain* and bring to the hearer's attention one aspect of the context only, namely the flower's state of fading. Presupposition, on the other hand, corresponds to the statement "p is implied by q" or "q implies p", denying only the possibility that p is true and q is false. A given interpretation of the picture (see departing train example) will hence exclude a whole range of possible interpretations of the utterance.

Different linkages between context and utterance will most likely make for different patterns of information processing (Fig. 1). A non-appropriate context is linked to the utterance by temporal proximity only (arrow a), and decoding of the utterance will therefore not be affected by the context at all. It seems reasonable to assume, moreover that a context will contribute most to message transmission when the linkage is one of presupposition (arrow 1). Context and utterance then are related at the level of cognitive representations as consecutive events (departing train—regret concerning late arrival). The context restricts the range of possible interpretations of the utterance. Moreover, the deictic word "*she*" will refer to some female person trying to catch a train, and

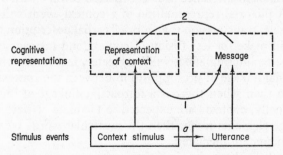

FIG. 1. Context-utterance linkages and patterns of information processing.

"*not . . . in time*" will immediately be decoded as related to the departure of that train. When there is a linkage of presupposition and implication, on the other hand, a relationship between context and message seems to be established by a retroactive process as well (arrows 1 and 2). In this case we have also to deal with two consecutive events. The context event, however, remains somewhat ambiguous until the utterance has been comprehended. Therefore, at the level of cognitive representations, the sequence (fading flower—insufficient light and heat) perhaps is most appropriately described as an event followed by an explanation.

A drawing extracts only some abstract features of a real-life situation. A single sentence describing the main features of that drawing is even more remote from the natural setting. In addition to other important differences, there is thus a step-wise decrease of details and a step-wise selective foregrounding of abstract features as we proceed from the actual scene of the train leaving the station via a drawing of that scene to the written sentence: "*The train left the station*". The pictorial representation provides a setting which most resembles the kind of natural settings for message transmission which were discussed above. For that reason, verbal context probably will contribute less to transmission of the message conveyed by the subsequent spoken utterance than a drawing portraying the same event. In addition, context and message elements are likely to fuse. Elements from the context may intrude in recall of the utterance whenever an appropriate context is provided. Such intrusions may occur in recall of regret concerning late arrival when the message is preceded by a drawing of a departing train. When asked only to reproduce the utterance, the hearer may be unable to separate what was *heard* from what was *seen*. Consequently he may end up with a reproduction such as "It's a pity she was late *for the train*". The probability of fusion of context event with verbally mediated message should be even greater, however, when both context and message are mediated by *words*.

The impact of an appropriate context upon decoding, storage, and retrieval of a spoken utterance thus is expected to vary with a number of conditions. A pictorial representation of a context event will contribute more to message transmission than a brief verbal description of the same event and will make for less fusion of context and message elements in memory. The facilitating effect will be greater, moreover, when there is a unidirectional linkage of presupposition between the context event and the utterance than when there is a retroactive linkage of implication as well. And, finally, contexts are expected to facilitate retrieval of higher-order message elements rather than the particular words by which such message elements are mediated.

The latter hypothesis implies that retrieval performance must be assessed in terms of higher-order content elements rather than verbatim reproduction of the utterance. More specifically, this means that the hypothesized context effects cannot be assessed adequately by measures of transitional errors in recall. An appropriate measure of message retrieval must be such that re-encodings like "*It's a pity . . .*", "*It's regrettable . . .*" and "*It's unfortunate . . .*" are accepted as recall of what was initially conveyed by "*It's a shame . . .*".

In order to predict specific effects of contexts upon retrieval performance it is necessary to specify how recall is to be assessed and the conditions under which retrieval will take place. For instance, recall may be prompted by providing the hearer with the beginning of the utterance to be reproduced or with one particular content word that appeared in it (Blumenthal, 1967). In principle either method allows for two very different strategies of retrieval. On the one hand reproduction of the remaining part of the utterance may be based upon rote memory. This means, more specifically, that perfect retrieval may mirror perfect

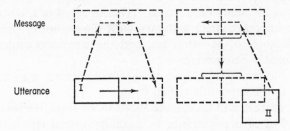

Message

Utterance

FIG. 2. Possible strategies of retrieval when (I) the beginning of the utterance and (II) a content clue phrase that did not appear in the utterance, are used to prompt recall.

retention of words and contingencies between words only without—in the extreme case—any comprehension of the message conveyed by the utterance at all. The prompting element, in addition to being an integral part of the sentence, is at the same time a clue to a higher-order message element. Retrieval thus may be dependent upon cohesion among message elements in memory, and reproduction of the remaining part of the utterance in the latter case will involve re-encoding. These extreme strategies are indicated in Fig. 2, I. The solid arrow represents some rote strategy, whereas the three broken arrows indicate a strategy of re-encoding.

When some content words from the initial utterance are used to prompt recall, verbatim reproduction in principle can either be due to rote retention of the utterance or, if there is a one-to-one correspondence between message elements and linguistic tools, to re-encoding of a perfectly retained message. A rote strategy is prohibited, however, if recall is prompted by some phrase that did not appear in the initial utterance at all. This will be the case, for instance, if recall of the utterance "*It's a shame she did not get there in time*" is prompted by the phrase "*too late*". The latter provides a clue to what was initially conveyed by "*not . . . in time*", and retrieval will, therefore, necessarily imply re-encoding as indicated in Fig. 2, II. Such a content clue will fail entirely if the utterance has been learned by rote only, without any comprehension of the message it conveyed. As a result, it is to be expected that the prompting method indicated in the latter example (and Fig. 2, II) should be particularly sensitive in assessing context effects upon retrieval performance.

The main outcome of our explorations of context and message transmission may now be expressed in a set of hypotheses.

1. Message transmission (decoding, storage and retrieval) will be facilitated when an utterance is preceded by some stimulus event which provides an appropriate context for it.
2. The appropriate context will enhance transmission of higher-order message elements rather than verbatim recall of the utterance.
3. Such a context effect will vary with the nature of the context, its relationship to the utterance, and the condition under which the utterance is being retrieved.
   (a) A pictorially presented context will enhance transmission more than a comparable verbal context.
   (b) A context will contribute more to message retrieval when it is linked to the utterance by a unidirectional relationship of presupposition only, than when there is also a retroactive linkage of implication between utterance and context.
   (c) The facilitating effect of context will be particularly strong when retrieval is prompted by some verbal element that, without having appeared in the stimulus utterance, provides a clue to its content.
4. When a given utterance is preceded by an appropriate context, elements from context and utterance will tend to fuse.
5. More context elements will intrude in recall of the utterance from a verbal context than from a comparable pictorially presented context.

THE EXPERIMENT

Methods

Experimental design. The experimental task was to listen to a set of eight unrelated, spoken utterances and to reproduce each of them as accurately as possible immediately afterwards. A slide was projected on a screen in front of the subject for four seconds; this was the signal for attention, informing the subject that the next utterance would follow immediately. Context was manipulated by varying the content of the slide. In the *non-appropriate context* condition (*NC*), arbitrarily chosen geometrical figures were used. In the *picture context* condition (*PC*), simple drawings of appropriate context events (such as a train leaving a station and a fading flower) served as ready signals. In the *verbal context* condition (*VC*), brief typewritten sentences describing the corresponding events appeared on the screen. Instructions and stimulus utterances were taped and were identical for all conditions. Differences between context conditions pertained exclusively to the stimulus event preceding each utterance.

Eight utterances were presented one after another. Then retrieval was assessed by two different prompting methods. Half of all subjects in each context condition were given the beginning of each stimulus utterance and asked to complete it. This condition will be referred to as *sentence completion* (*SC*). The other half were given a content clue that had not appeared in the stimulus utterance. This sub-condition will be referred to as *content clue* retrieval (*CC*). In addition, two different orders of prompting (O_1 and O_2) were used; both orders deviated from the initial order of presentation of the eight utterances.

The linkages between context and utterance, moreover, were of two different kinds. Half of the utterances were linked to their appropriate contexts by *presupposition* only, the other half were hypothesized to involve a retroactive process of *implication* as well. This distinction has been discussed earlier, and the essential difference is indicated by arrows 1 and 2 in Fig. 1.

The distribution of subjects over sub-conditions is shown in Table 1. The two types of context-utterance linkage are a within-subject source of variance and, for that reason, not represented in Table 1. The complete design is thus a $3 \times 2 \times 2 \times 2$ factorial design, with three context conditions (*VC/NC/PC*), two retrieval conditions (*SC/CC*), two

TABLE 1

Experimental design

		Contexts					
		VC		*NC*		*PC*	
Order of retrieval		O_1	O_2	O_1	O_2	O_1	O_2
	SC	10	10	10	10	10	10
Retrieval condition	*CC*	10	10	10	10	10	10

orders of retrieval (O_1/O_2), and two types of context-utterance linkage (Implication/Presupposition).

The major dependent measures were derived from recall of the eight stimulus utterances. In addition, a second recall task was introduced in all sub-conditions. The subject was given the stimulus utterances, again in a random order, and in each case was asked what had appeared on the screen immediately before that utterance. This second task will be referred to as *recall of ready signals.*

Stimulus material. The experiment was conducted in Dutch. English translations of the eight utterances in the order they were presented are given in Table 2; the original Dutch versions are added in parentheses. The ready signals in *PC* were simple drawings of (1) a fading flower, (2) a train leaving a station, (3) a TV set with a price tag, (4) a lady buying candles, (5) a hand knocking at a door, (6) a factory looking as if it is falling down, (7) a man knocking with a stick on a ceiling, and (8) a big fish catching bait.

A vertical line divides each utterance into two parts, the beginning and the ending. The first part was used to prompt recall in the sentence completion retrieval condition. It will be noted that every sentence beginning conveys a message element that may be expressed in a number of alternative ways as well. Thus the beginnings of the first and the sixth utterances both express *insufficiency*, the second and the fifth convey *regret*, the third and the eighth share an element of *high probability*, whereas the fourth and the seventh utterances both convey an initial element of *high frequency*. The endings, on the other hand, are constructed in such a way as to counteract confusion among utterances; no content element in any single ending appears in any one of the remaining seven utterances. Four of the utterances, moreover, were supposed to be linked to their appropriate contexts by *presupposition* only. These are the second, the third, the fifth and the eighth utterance. The remaining four utterances (numbers one, four, six and seven) were supposed to be linked to their contexts by a retroactive process of *implication* as well.

Subjects. The subjects in the experiment were 120 Belgian soldiers from the Kwartier Cdt Hemptinne in Heverlee. They were very homogeneous with respect to educational background, having on the average one-and-a-half years of lower education beyond the elementary school level.

The soldiers came to the Laboratory for Experimental Social Psychology of the Psychological Institute of the University of Louvain where the experiment was carried out as part of a training seminar in experimental social psychology.

Procedure. The subjects were run in six groups of twenty each. Order

TABLE 2
Stimulus utterances and content clue prompts in Dutch and English

Ready signal	Utterance	Content clue
VC *The plant is dying.* (De plant sterft af)	1. *There was insufficient/light and heat.* (Er was onvol- doende/licht en warmte)	*Dark and cold.* (Donker en koud)
NC Trapezium		
VC *The train left the station.* (De trein verliet het station)	2. *It's a shame/she did not get there in time.* (Het is zonde dat/ze niet op tijd daar was)	*Too late.* (Te laat)
NC Cross		
VC *The TV set is very expensive.* (Het TV- toestel is zeer duur)	3. *He very likely will/not be able to keep up the pay- ments.* (Zeer waar- schijnlijk zal hij/het niet kunnen afbetalen)	*Costs too much.* (Kost te veel)
NC Semi-circle		
VC *The lady is buying candles.* (De dam koopt kaarsen)	4. *Every day there are/break- downs in the electricity.* (Elke dag zijn er/pannes in de elektriciteit)	*Power cuts.* (Stroomonder- brekingen)
NC Square		
VC *Somebody knocked at the door.* (Iemand klopte aan de deur)	5. *It is a pity/she was not at home.* (Het is jammer dat/ze niet thuis was)	*Absent.* (Afwezig)
NC Star		
VC *The factory was derelict.* (De fabriek was vervallen)	6. *There was not enough/gain from the production.* (Er was niet genoeg/winst op de productie)	*Little profit.* (Weinig profijt)
NC Rectangle		
VC *The man is knocking with a stick on the ceiling.* (De man klopt met een stok tegen de zoldering)	7. *All the time there are/ people making noise above.* (Voortdurend zijn er/boven mensen lawaai aan het maken)	*Din.* (Kabaal)
NC Circle		
VC *The bait is taken by a big fish.* (Een grote vis bijt in het aas)	8. *He probably will/break his line.* (Denkelijk zal hij/zijn lijn breken)	*Something snaps.* (Iets gaat stuk)
NC Triangle		

of retrieval was controlled by preparing two different versions of response booklets, one for each half of a group. The two orders (O_1 and O_2 in Table 1), which were reversals of one another, were set up in such a way that mean number of activities intervening between presentation and recall was the same for presuppostion and implication items.

The experiment was introduced as a study of recall of spoken utter- ances. Instructions for the listening task were tape-recorded and identical for all groups. They emphasized the importance of attentive listening and stressed accuracy of recall. The light was switched off while the subjects were listening, and the slides were explicitly introduced as ready signals for the utterances to be recalled. Two of the slide-spoken utterance combinations were presented as examples in order to make the subjects familiar with the task, to show them the type of relationship between ready signal and utterance in advance. Each slide was projected for four seconds, and the utterance followed the moment the ready signal disappeared. The interval between projections of ready signals was seven seconds.

Tape-recorded instructions for retrieval followed immediately after the last stimulus utterance, and one of the introductory examples was used to explain the recall task in detail. The subject was instructed to proceed page by page in his response booklet, and he was given 25 seconds to write down his reproduction of each utterance. Each page of the response booklet contained the prompting element for one utterance only, a *sentence beginning* in the sentence completion condition and the corresponding *content clue* in the content clue condition.

Coding, recall measures, and predictions. A complete dictionary of all content elements in the stimulus material was prepared. This dictionary contained (1) the exact Dutch word or phrase for the content element, (2) an English translation of it, and (3) its exact location in the stimulus material, specifying in *which item* it appeared, whether it had appeared in *the beginning* or *the ending of the stimulus utterance itself*, in *the verbal or pictorial context for it*, or in *the content clue*.

A list of synonyms for all content elements was prepared after a careful analysis of all retrieval responses. The list was prepared with the assistance of three Dutch-English bilinguals and Froimont's "Dictionnaire des synonymes, Français-Néerlandais" and organized in the same way as the dictionary of content elements. Responses from all three context conditions were scrambled, and coding was carried out as a strictly mechanical procedure by team members who had no knowledge of Dutch prior to the investigation. Every successive word in the Dutch reproduction was checked against the alphabetically ordered dictionary and list of synonyms. Neither deictic words ("he", "there") nor connectives ("was", "is") were included in the final recall measures.

Every reproduction of *a sentence ending* was then scored with respect to accurate recall, synonymy, and intrusion from context. A score of 1 for *accurate recall* was assigned if one or more content elements appeared in exactly the same form as in the stimulus utterance, provided that no other content element from the sentence ending was given back in a synonymous form. If such was the case *or* if no content element from the stimulus utterance was reproduced at all, a score of 0 for accurate recall was assigned. A score of 1 for *synonymy* was assigned, if, and only if, at least one appropriate synonym appeared in the reproduction. A score of 1 for *semantically correct recall*, moreover, was assigned, if, and only if, at least one content element was given back accurately or in a synonymous form. The scores were thus either 1 or 0 for accurate recall, synonymy, and semantically correct recall. *Intrusions from context* were counted separately.

Sentence beginnings were scored in the same way. A score of 1 for semantically correct recall would thus mean that the content element of the sentence beginning had been given back, either accurately or by means of a synonymous expression. The score for semantically correct recall of *the whole utterance* in the content clue retrieval condition was then simply computed as the sum of the scores for sentence beginning and end, *provided that the subject had not given back exclusively wrong content elements in the sentence ending.* This additional provision was necessary in order to prevent clear-cut cases of fusion of different stimulus utterances from being scored as semantically correct recall. If utterance "*It's a shame she did not get there in time*" was given back as "*It's a shame he could not pay for it*", a score of 0 for semantically correct recall of the whole utterance thus was assigned. The maximum score is 2 (at least one semantically correct element from each part of the utterance). These scores which were strictly defined by the dictionary of content elements, the list of synonyms, and the rules stated above, were checked against independent subjective judgments of retrieval performance by two Dutch-speaking judges. Finally, recall of ready signals was coded by having two judges independently check every response against the eight different context stimuli.

Predictions of retrieval were derived from the hypotheses presented on p. 36. An analysis of variance of *semantically correct recall* of sentence endings thus was expected to yield a significant main effect of context, the expected order of performance being $PC > VC > NC$ (Hypotheses 1 and 3a). Type of linkage, however, has no meaning when utterances are preceded by arbitrary geometrical forms and therefore should make a difference only when an appropriate context is provided (in PC and VC). Hence, the effect should come out as an interaction effect of item type × context, presupposition items being expected to be particularly well recalled in PC and VC (Hypothesis 3b). Since appropriate contexts were expected to make for a higher level of processing and content clues were supposed to force the subject to re-encode higher-order message elements, a significant interaction of context × retrieval condition was expected as well (Hypothesis 3c). Recall thus should be particularly good in *PC*, *CC* and *VC*, *CC*. The greatest context effect according to these predictions should be observed when a pictorial context is linked to the utterance by presupposition and retrieval is prompted by a content clue. The greatest difference with respect to semantically correct recall of sentence endings should accordingly be the difference between *PC*, *CC*, Presupposition and *NC*, *CC*, Presupposition.

According to what has been said above, an analysis of variance of semantically correct recall of the whole utterances (for content clue retrieval only) should yield a strong main effect of context and a significant interaction effect of context × type of linkage. Moreover, the hypothesis concerning context and level of processing (Hypothesis 2) implies that the ratio of synonyms to accurate recall should be higher when an appropriate context is provided. However, a comparison of context conditions with respect to ratio of synonyms would be appropriate only in the content clue retrieval condition, since only sentence beginnings had been constructed with a systematic one-to-many relationship between message element and linguistic tools. On the other hand, intrusions from contexts in the recall of utterances were expected to appear primarily in sentence endings and to be more frequent in *VC* than in *PC* conditions (Hypotheses 4 and 5).

Recall of ready signals was supposed to serve partly as a check upon manipulation of contexts; the more intimately a context stimulus is related to the utterance, the greater the probability that it will be recalled when the utterance is presented. Recall was thus expected to be good for the appropriate contexts *PC* and *VC*, but very poor for *NC*.

Results

Two items had to be discarded in the final measures of retrieval performance. These were *utterance four* ("Every day there are/breakdowns in the electricity") and *utterance eight* ("He will probably/break his line"). The Dutch content clue for the latter is "*Iets gaat stuk*" ("*something breaks*"). This turned out to be a perfectly appropriate clue for *utterance four* as well. All analyses of retrieval performance were consequently based upon six items only, the implication items *one, six,* and *seven* and the presupposition items *two, three* and *five* (see Table 2).

Two judges rated retention of *utterance five* ("*It is a pity/she was not at home*") and *utterance seven* ("*All the time there are/people making noise above*") on a five point scale, ranging from 0 (no recall) to 4 (perfect retention of the utterance). The relationship between mean subjective ratings and objective scores of semantically correct recall is shown in

TABLE 3

Correspondence between subjective judgment and objective coding of recall

Subjective judgment	Objective scores		
	0	1	2
3·0–3·0	0	18	16
1·5–2·5	1	18	8
0·0–1·0	57	2	0

Table 3, and the observed correspondence yields a coefficient of contingency of 0·70. Discrepancies are due in part to the fact that sentence endings vary with respect to number of content elements, whereas maximal contribution to objective recall score of any ending is 1.

The main results concerning retrieval performance are presented in Fig. 3 and Tables 4 and 5. Figure 3 shows retrieval performance for implication and presupposition items for each of the six experimental groups when order of retrieval is ignored. Maximal achievement with respect to semantically correct recall of sentence endings for every group is thus subjects × items, i.e. $20 \times 3 = 60$. The same is true for sentence beginnings. Actual achievement is the sum of verbatim reproductions and synonyms. The outstanding performance with respect to retrieval of *sentence endings* is thus recall of presupposition items by subjects who had pictorial contexts and retrieval was prompted by content clues (see right hand bottom column in Fig. 1).

An analysis of variance of sentence ending retrieval is presented in Table 4. The analysis yields four significant main effects, i.e. context, retrieval condition, order of retrieval and item type all contribute significantly to recall of sentence endings. An inspection of Fig. 3 shows that the context effect stems exclusively from the over-all superiority of *PC*. The mean score for the *PC* group is 2·1, whereas the *VC* and *NC* group both have mean scores of 1·4. The significant interaction of context by item type ($C \times I$) and the significant triple interaction of context, retrieval and item type ($C \times R \times I$), moreover, stem from the fact that retrieval of presupposition items is particularly good among subjects in the *PC* condition and from the fact that content clues selectively facilitate their retrieval of presupposition items. This comes out clearly in a comparison of the four *PC* columns for retrieval of sentence endings in Fig. 3. Retrieval of implication utterances stays the same across the two different prompting methods, whereas semantically correct recall of presupposition endings is exactly three times as good under content clue

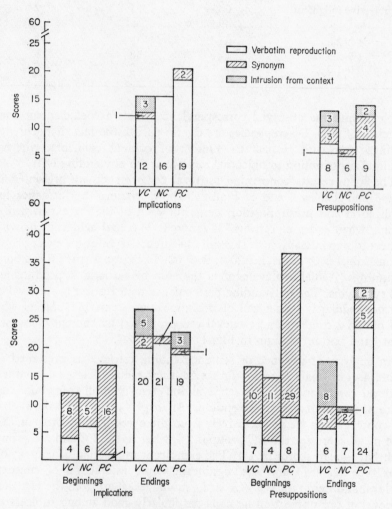

FIG. 3. Recall performance.
A. Sentence completion groups. B. Content clue retrieval groups.

TABLE 4

Analysis of variance, all conditions, semantically correct recall of sentence endings

Source	df	Ss	MS	F	P
C (contexts, $VC/NC/PC$)	2	6·56	3·28	4·93	<0·01
P (retrieval, SC/CC)	1	4·00	4·00	6·02	<0·025
O (order of retrieval, O_1/O_2)	1	3·04	3·04	4·57	<0·05
$C \times R$	2	0·41	0·20	0·31	
$C \times O$	2	0·68	0·34	0·51	
$R \times O$	1	0·10	0·10	0·16	
$C \times R \times O$	2	0·06	0·03	0·04	
s.w. (CRO)	108	71·83	0·67	—	
I (item type, Implication/ Presupposition)	1	5·10	5·10	9·28	<0·01
$C \times I$	2	3·40	1·70	3·10	=0·05
$R \times I$	1	0·04	0·04	0·07	
$O \times I$	1	0·70	0·70	1·30	
$C \times R \times I$	2	5·03	2·51	4·57	<0·025
$C \times O \times I$	2	0·76	0·38	0·69	
$R \times O \times I$	1	0·10	0·10	0·19	
$C \times R \times O \times I$	2	0·51	0·25	0·46	
s.w. (CRO) $\times I$	108	59·43	0·55		

TABLE 5

Analysis of variance, semantically correct recall, content clue retrieval

Source	df	Ss	MS	F	P
C (contexts, $VC/NC/PC$)	2	16·55	8·28	8·47	<0·01
O (order of retrieval, O_1/O_2)	1	1·01	1·01	1·03	
$C \times O$	2	1·22	0·61	0·62	
s.w. (CO)	54	52·78	0·98		
I (item type, Implication/ Presupposition)	1	0·21	0·21	0·23	
$C \times I$	2	14·52	7·26	8·12	<0·01
$O \times I$	1	0·08	0·08	0·08	
$C \times O \times I$	2	0·45	0·23	0·25	
s.w. (CO) $\times I$	54	48·28	0·89		

retrieval as when the beginnings of the utterances are used to prompt recall.

An item-by-item comparison of *PC* and *NC* with respect to recall of sentence endings in the content clue condition shows that there is no overlap between presupposition items on the one hand and implication items on the other; all presupposition items are better recalled in *PC*, and the smallest positive difference between *PC* and *NC* for any pre-supposition item exceeds the greatest positive difference for any impli-cation item. The same holds true when a strictly analogous comparison between *PC* and *VC* is carried out. This means that items representing the same type of linkage in the *PC* condition behaved in the same way, i.e. that the superiority reflected in the bottom right hand column in Fig. 3 must be attributed to *type of linkage* rather than to any unique picture-utterance constellation.

Semantically correct recall of whole utterances can only be assessed when retrieval is prompted by content clues. A separate analysis of variance for retrieval performance, therefore, was conducted on the content clue groups separately. The results are presented in Table 5. As in the preceding analysis, a strong main effect of context is observed. This effect stems again exclusively from superior performances by *CC* subjects in the *PC* condition, the mean scores being 3·2 for the *PC* condition and 1·3 for the *VC* + *NC* conditions. More than twice as much was thus retrieved when pictorial contexts were provided. The strong interaction effect of context × item type, moreover, means that there was a selective facilitation of utterances linked to pictorial contexts by presupposition, mean scores for presupposition items being 2·1 for *PC*; 0·6 for *VC*; and 0·5 for *NC*.

Ratios of synonymous to verbatim reproductions of sentence beginnings are given in Table 6. *PC* comes out with the highest ratio of synonyms in all comparisons between conditions, with *only one verbatim reproduction*

TABLE 6

Verbatim (v) and synonymous (s) reproductions of sentence beginnings

Items	Contexts					
	VC		*NC*		*PC*	
	v	*s*	*v*	*s*	*v*	*s*
Imp	4	8	6	5	1	16
Pres	7	10	4	11	8	29
All	11	18	10	16	9	45

per five appropriate synonymous expressions given back on the average. When Fischer's exact probability test was applied to retrieval of all sentence beginnings in the three context conditions (see bottom row of Table 5), the following p-values were obtained: VC versus NC, $p = 0.63$; PC versus NC, $p = 0.03$; and PC versus $VC = 0.03$. Ratio of synonymous to verbatim reproductions thus was nearly identical for subjects in the VC and NC groups, whereas pictorial contexts yielded a significantly higher ratio of synonymous reproductions than either one of the other two context conditions.

An alternate analysis was used in an attempt to compare subjects' tendency toward rote learning, where each word is the cue for the next, as against meaningful learning and recall, where the sentence is reconstructed from memory of the content. The score chosen to reflect rote learning was the number of words reproduced correctly, where each word follows from the previous one (Score A). If the first word of the phrase or sentence is given correctly, *and as the first word*, the subject scores one. Then if the second word is given, *as the second word*, the subject scores two, and so on. Each additional word correctly given, and in the correct order, scores one. Once an incorrect word has occurred or a word has occurred in the wrong place, the subject stops scoring. The score selected as reflecting meaningful learning was number of words reproduced *regardless of order* (Score B). Each correct word reproduced, regardless of order, scores one. Separate scores are calculated for the first and second halves of the sentences in the CC conditions. Comparison of these two scores for the various conditions shows how much recall of each type occurred in each condition. It also provides a good index of how much was recalled overall and how much of the second part of the sentence was recalled. It also allows some comparison to be made between the SC and CC conditions.

Table 7 shows that recall is superior in all CC conditions, as against all SC conditions. This is particularly impressive since subjects had more to remember in the CC conditions. Evidently recall is easier when a "meaningful" cue is given.

Also recall is superior in the PC conditions, regardless of recall condition, which suggests that a "meaningful" context is an additional factor which assists recall. The NC and VC conditions do not differ greatly.

Table 8 shows that the ratio of Score A to Score B was lowest in CC conditions, especially VC and PC. This suggests that meaningful recall conditions facilitate non-rote recall. Note also that the lowest ratio is in the PC/CC and VC/CC conditions, where encoding and recall are likely to occur at a meaningful level, whereas in NC/SC, which most favours non-meaningful recall, we have the highest ratio of A to B. However, the

TABLE 7

Recall second half

	PC	VC	NC	
CC	200	124	97	421
SC	123	81	82	286
	323	205	179	707

TABLE 8

Ratio of exact reproductions/total reproductions

	PC	VC	NC	
CC	$\frac{60}{314}$ (19%)	$\frac{36}{197}$ (18%)	$\frac{45}{177}$ (25%)	21%
SC	$\frac{60}{123}$ (49%)	$\frac{38}{81}$ (49%)	$\frac{45}{82}$ (55%)	51%

SC and CC groups are not strictly comparable. The SC groups have less to remember and so are more likely to remember everything exactly whereas the CC groups have longer sentences to remember and are therefore more likely to rephrase them.

Intrusions of context elements in retrieval of utterances were few in number (see Fig. 3). When they do occur they occur most frequently among VC subjects and are particularly frequent when presupposition items are retrieved on the basis of content clues. Overall performance of VC subjects under this latter condition is poor, with subjects giving back almost as many context elements as appropriate elements from the sentence endings.

Recall of ready signals is presented in Table 9. The two independent

TABLE 9

Per cent correct recall of ready signals

Retrieval	VC	Contexts NC	PC
SC	51·9	13·6	78·3
CC	28·8	11·9	75·5

judges showed agreement on 98% of all judgments and the few cases of disagreement were resolved by introducing a third judge. Table 9 shows that picture contexts were extremely well recalled, that recall of verbal contexts was fairly good, and that non-appropriate contexts were very poorly recalled. The *VC* subjects had a particularly poor recall of contexts after content clue retrieval of utterances. A comparison of *VC*, *SC* and *VC*, *CC* yields a highly significant difference ($X^2 = 17 \cdot 78$; $df = 1$; $p = 0 \cdot 001$), whereas the differences between *PC*, *SC/PC*, *CC* and *NC*, *SC/NC*, *CC* respectively are negligible.

Discussion

Table 4 shows a significant main effect of *item type*, implication items on the whole being recalled far better than presupposition items. This difference is also observed in the *NC* conditions (see Fig. 3), in which utterances are linked to context stimuli by temporal proximity alone. Therefore it is obvious that the significant effect of item type has nothing to do with the predicted effect of *implication and presupposition types of linkage* between context and utterance. It so happens that the implication *utterances* are better retained in memory even when no appropriate contexts are provided for them.

The main effect of item type may also possibly illuminate some subtle relationships between context and utterance that were discussed in the introduction. Three implication utterances were included in the final analysis, (1) *"There was insufficient/light and heat"*, (6) *"There was not enough/gain from the production"*, and (7) *"All the time there are/people making noise above"*. The presupposition utterances were (2) *"It's a shame/ she did not get there in time"*, (3) *"He very likely will/not be able to keep up the payments"* and (5) *"It is a pity/she was not at home"*. These six utterances differ in a variety of ways, but there are nevertheless some common features within each set and some differences between the two sets that should be observed.

The main noun phrase in every implication item is a content word or phrase in the sentence ending (*"light and heat"*, *"gain"*, *"people"*). The three presupposition utterances, on the other hand, are all about persons, and a deictic word (*"she"*, *"He"*, and *"she"*) serves in every case as the noun phrase to which the content elements of the sentence ending are linked. It appears, therefore, as if implication items are more autonomous, i.e. *less in need of context events*, than presupposition items. More specifically, a higher degree of autonomy means that less additional information seems to be required in order to decide which higher-order message elements are being conveyed. Utterances linked to contexts by presupposition were hypothesized to be clarified by the contexts. This means that the utterance in isolation must be somewhat ambiguous. Thus what is suggested as a topic for further inquiry is a built-in correlation between autonomy of utterances and type of context-utterance linkage in everyday verbal communication.

The fact that content clues yielded better recall of sentence endings than sentence completion makes it clear that in no sub-condition did subjects resort to extreme rote strategies of storage and retrieval. The difference between retrieval conditions, however, should also be viewed against the systematic one-to-two relationship between sentence beginnings and sentence endings; a content clue is always (once utterances *four* and *eight* are discarded) a clue to one and only one unique utterance, whereas every sentence beginning conveys a message element that appeared in two different stimulus utterances.

Different orders of retrieval were introduced as a safeguard against possible contaminations of predicted effects by serial order. O_2 is simply the reversal of O_1 (see Table 1), and the main effect of order therefore means only that one order of prompting turned out to yield significantly better retrieval than its reverse. This may serve as a reminder that retrieval performance in a laboratory recall task such as the one employed in the present experiment is affected by a number of factors other than those that were made the focus of theoretical analysis in the present study. What is more comforting, however, is the fact that *order of retrieval is not involved in any even remotely significant interaction effect*. The impact of all theoretically significant variables upon retrieval performance remained essentially the same whether recall of the eight stimulus utterances was prompted in one particular order or in its reverse.

The theoretically most significant variables are (see Table 4) *context*, *context × item type*, and *context × retrieval × item type*. The significant main effect of context, as already indicated, is entirely due to the over-all superiority of *PC* subjects over *VC* and *NC* subjects. Hypothesis 1 (p. 36) hence must be said to be only partially confirmed; message transmission was only facilitated by appropriate *pictorial contexts*. Hypothesis 3 (a) that picture contexts enhance transmission significantly more than comparable verbal contexts consequently is already confirmed. Hypothesis 3 (b) holds true only for *PC*; the significant *context × item type* interaction is due to the fact that *NC* and *VC* subjects had a far better recall of implication endings than of presupposition endings, whereas *PC* subjects recalled more of presupposition endings on the average (see Table 4).

Hypothesis 3 (c) asserts that context effects should be particularly strong when retrieval is prompted by content clues. The *context × retrieval* interaction is negligible, however, and the general hypothesis concerning context and retrieval condition, irrespective of type of linkage, hence must be rejected. The significant *context × retrieval × item type* interaction effect means, however, that the hypothesized relationship holds true *if and only if the linkage is one of presupposition.* The significant triple interaction is thus mainly a statistical reflection of the remarkably high column in the lower right corner of Fig. 3.

As far as retrieval of sentence endings is concerned, by far the strongest context effect is observed *when a pictorial context is linked to the utterance by presupposition and message retrieval is prompted by a content clue that did not appear in the utterance* (Hypotheses 3 a–c). Therefore what was hypothesized about *appropriate contexts,* according to Table 4 and Fig. 3 appears to hold true only for *picture contexts,* and the expected interaction effect of context and retrieval condition has only been observed when context stimulus was linked to the utterance by a unidirectional relationship of presupposition.

These interpretations are further corroborated by the analysis of semantically correct recall of whole utterances in the content clue conditions (Table 5). An analysis of variance brings out two clearly significant effects, both of which were predicted. There is, first of all, a significant main effect of context, *PC* being far superior to *VC* and *NC* (see Fig. 3). The only other significant effect is the *context × item type* interaction. Therefore Table 4 provides unequivocal evidence in support of the modified Hypotheses 1 and 3 (b). Message transmission (decoding, storage, and retrieval) has been facilitated when utterances were preceded by appropriate pictorial contexts only, and such pictorial contexts contributed more to message retrieval when they were linked to utterances by a unidirectional relationship of presupposition than when a retroactive linkage of implication was involved as well.

What was predicted concerning appropriate contexts and re-encoding of message elements, moreover, holds true for pictorial contexts only (see Hypothesis 2, p. 36). The observed ratio of synonyms to verbatim reproductions of sentence beginnings was significantly higher in the picture context condition than in either of the two other context groups (see Table 5). The key Dutch word for the message element of *regret* in utterance two, for instance, was "*zonde*". Only two *PC* subjects gave back "zonde", whereas two subjects used the word "jammer", and eight subjects expressed regret by the key word "spijtig". Both of the latter words are perfectly appropriate tools for conveying regret. The high frequency of such synonyms in the *PC* condition provides fairly unequivocal evidence that a higher level of processing and hence a stronger component of re-encoding in the retrieval situation were induced by pictorial contexts.

/ 82781

The major differences between what were supposed to be *appropriate verbal contexts* and *non-appropriate contexts* appear therefore to pertain to fusion of context and utterance (see intrusions in Fig. 3) and recall of context stimuli (see Table 9). The intrusion of elements from the verbal contexts in recall of utterances and the fairly good recall of verbal contexts when subjects were asked what appeared on the screen immediately before the utterance, show that the verbal contexts were appropriate in certain important respects. From certain points of view they were even more unequivocally related to the utterances than the corresponding drawings. For instance, the ambiguity of the context event of the fading flower is considerably reduced as we proceed from the drawing to the written sentence "The plant is dying".[a] A process of retroactive disambiguation, a refocusing upon that aspect of the context event which is explained by the subsequent utterance, hence should apply primarily to *pictorial contexts* which are linked to utterances by implication. Pretests of pictorial contexts indicated that this is the case. The subjects were simply asked to describe what they saw in the drawings. When a drawing appeared in isolation, a number of aspects were mentioned. On the other hand, the feature of particular contextual relevance sometimes was not mentioned at all. When subjects were listening to the stimulus utterance for a given pictorial context while describing the drawing, however, they tended to organize their description more around the features representing the context for the utterance.

The absence of facilitating effects of verbal contexts upon message transmission in this study is thus difficult to explain. Verbal contexts appear to be perfectly appropriate in certain respects, and, to the extent that data on intrusions and recall of ready signals can be brought in as evidence, even appear to be linked to the utterances in memory. Thus they are clearly more appropriate than the geometrical figures in the *NC* condition, even though they contribute no more to semantically correct recall.

These apparently contradictory findings may possibly be explained by returning to the introductory considerations concerning rote learning of utterances versus natural settings for message transmission. What is achieved by the introduction of verbal contexts, in a way, is an extension of the spoken utterance by adding an additional written beginning rather than a modification of the listening situation in the direction of a natural communication setting. Moreover, the cohesion of verbal context and utterance in memory is significantly more reduced by an intervening retrieval activity based on content clues than one involving sentence

---

[a] "De plant" in Dutch is the most appropriate label for "flower-in-pot", and the phrase has no polysemy involving *industrial plant*.

completion (see Table 9). This suggests that the connection between context and utterance in the verbal context condition may be established in part below the level of higher-order message elements after all. The process of re-encoding induced by the content clue retrieval task has apparently disrupted the association between the written context and the immediately following utterance. The present experiment does not provide data which allow for a comparison between processing of utterances in natural message transmission settings and rote learning of utterances. All experimental conditions (even the sub-condition in which geometrical figures served as ready signals and retrieval was tested by sentence completion) are far removed from the typical rote learning situation. The impact of repetition and overlearning upon level of processing, however, may possible be explored by expanding the *NC, SC* and *NC, CC* conditions of the present study into learning situations. The two retrieval methods may be introduced at a stage of extreme overlearning. Success in *sentence completion* and failure in *content clue retrieval*, for instance, would then indicate a very low level of processing, possibly analogous to the state of semantic satiation caused by prolonged repetition of single words.

What may be safely concluded on the basis of the present study, however, is that *one-trial learning of meaningful sentences* involves cognitive processes over and beyond storage of "syntactic footnotes" and formation of connections between *syntactically defined* "nodes" or "encoding steps". The most unequivocal evidence for this conclusion stems from two observations, namely the very high over-all frequency of synonymous expressions in retrieval of sentence beginnings and the fact that retrieval was very successfully prompted by elements that did not appear in the stimulus utterances at all. The subjects in all conditions listened with a set for accurate recall, and the request for accuracy was repeated in the instruction for the retrieval task. What was being stored and retrieved, however, were apparently neither the stimulus words nor syntactically defined clusters of such words, but rather some as yet very poorly understood outputs of a decoding process which have been tentatively described as higher-order message elements.

This is clearly seen if, instead of our present assessment of retrieval of message elements, we examine occurrence of *verbatim reproduction of stimulus utterances* in a strict left-to-right sequence. If the first-appearing transitional error is made the criterion for failure, we end up with a recall score of zero for nearly every subject. Content elements in sentence endings thus are almost always reached via routes other than their direct connections to the exact stimulus words in sentence beginnings (see Fig. 3, lower columns).

LORETTE WILMOT LIBRARY
NAZARETH COLLEGE

Retrieval performance, however, may reflect more abstract syntactic connections, and we might try to examine relationships between *prompting element* and *stimulus utterance* in a way similar to Blumenthal's analysis of prompted recall (Blumenthal, 1967). For instance, consider Utterance 1 (*"Er was onvoldoende/licht en warmte"* with content clue *"Donker en koud"*) and Utterance 6 (*"Er was niet genoeg/winst op de productie"*, with content clue *"Weinig profijt"*). When the content clue is used to prompt recall, retrieval performance is very similar for these two utterances. Retrieval of Utterance 1 is significantly better under the *SC* condition than under the *CC* condition, whereas the reverse is true for Utterance 6. These findings may possibly be interpreted as reflecting different syntactic connections between sentence beginning and sentence ending in the two cases. The element of insufficiency (*"onvoldoende"*) in Utterance 1 is tied to two juxtaposed content elements in the ending, namely *"licht"* and *"warmte"* and may be said to be a "logical predicate" of both of them. The corresponding element in Sentence 2 (*"niet genoeg"*) on the other hand, is tied to the whole phrase *"winst op de productie"* and has hence no direct "logical predicate"-relationship to the content element *"productie"*. It should be noted, moreover, that the greatest discrepancy between the two retrieval conditions *SC/CC* is found for Utterance 7 (*"Voortdurend zijn er/boven mensen lawaai an het maken"* with content clue *"Kabaal"*). The strikingly inferior recall in all three context conditions when retrieval is prompted by sentence beginning may perhaps be explained by the fact that the beginning in these cases contains only an adverbial, a rather peripherally located element of the content structure of the utterance.

A strikingly inferior recall under the *SC* condition, however, is also observed for Utterance 3 (*"Zeer waarschijnlijk zal hij/het niet kunnen afbetalen"*, with content clue *"Kost te veel"*). Recall is at least four times better both in *PC*, *NC*, and *VC* when the content clue is given as a prompting element. In this case, however, the sentence beginning contains the element *"hij"*, which constitutes *the main noun phrase* of the utterance according to its surface structure as well as the *"logical subject"* element of its deep structure. The content clue, on the other hand, has apparently no slot in the utterance at all, neither at its superficial nor deep level. What is conveyed by the stimulus utterance is *high probability of failure to keep up payments*, and such a state of affairs may very likely be related to *poverty* on the part of the purchaser or *high price*, for example. In this case the content clue seems to facilitate reproduction in a very subtle way, not via its connection with the message conveyed by the stimulus utterance itself, but rather via what was spontaneously *inferred* by the hearer on the basis of that message. What is clearly extrinsic

LORETTE WILMOT LIBRARY
NAZARETH COLLEGE

relative to the stimulus utterance seems to be a far better prompting element than a part of the utterance itself, even a part containing its "logical subject".

The preceding analysis of syntactic relations is purely casuistic. Utterances and content clues were not constructed with such a syntactic analysis in mind, and a systematic approach as developed by Blumenthal (1967) therefore was not possible. This casuistic analysis corroborates, however, the conclusions derived from our main analysis of retrieval performance. Word-to-word connections and specific relationships between syntactically defined elements of the stimulus utterance do not provide us with very helpful clues to retrieval performance, not even when the utterances to be recalled were presented without any appropriate contexts (in *NC*).

The subordinate role of particular linguistic tools is most clearly demonstrated in the present study when utterances are being processed in appropriate pictorial contexts, that is when retrieval of *what was said* is facilitated by *what was seen*. The effects of such contexts, moreover, appear to be particularly strong when there is a unidirectional relationship of presupposition between context and utterance. The two types of context-utterance linkages in the present experiment were, however, only very vaguely defined, and construction of context stimuli and utterances to be recalled hence were to a large extent based upon intuition.

A more systematic investigation of type of linkage may be attempted in future studies. For instance, a picture context condition may be elaborated into two sub-conditions by presenting every utterance in connection with two different pictures, one picture establishing a linkage of presupposition and the other one of implication. The introductory theoretical analysis and the findings from the present study represent only a preliminary exploratory and adventurous step into a largely unknown area of research.

REFERENCES

Blumenthal, A. L. (1967). Prompted recall of sentences, *J. verb. Learn. verb Behav.* **6,** 203–206.

Chomsky, N. (1957). "Syntactic Structures," Mouton, The Hague.

Ducrot, O. (1966). Logique et linguistique, *Language* **2,** 16–21.

Johnson, N. F. (1965). Linguistic models and functional units of language behavior. *In* "Directions in Psycholinguistics" (S. Rosenberg, ed.). Macmillan, New York.

Kolers, P. (1965). Bilingual facilitation of short term memory words remembered with respect to semantic rather than morphemic properties. Paper presented at the EPA meeting in Atlantic City, New Jersey.

Mehler, J. and Miller, G. A. (1964). Retroactive interference in the recall of simple sentences. *Br. J. Psychol.* **55,** 295–301.

Reichling, A. (1963). Das Problem der Bedeutung in der Sprachwissenschaft. Innsbrucker Beiträge zur Kulturwissenschaft, Sonderheft 19. Innsbruck.

Rommetveit, R. (1968). "Words, Meanings and Messages," Academic Press, New York and London.

Savin, H. and Perchonock, E. (1965). Grammatical structure and the immediate recall of English sentences, *J. verb. Learn. verb. Behav.* **4,** 348–353.

Tannenbaum, P. H. and Williams, F. (Spring, 1966). Personal communication.

Uhlenbeck, E. M. (1963). An appraisal of transformation theory, *Lingua* **12,** 1–18.

Processing of Utterances in Contexts *versus* Rote Learning of Sentences: Some Pilot Studies and a Design for an Experiment

ROLV MIKKEL BLAKAR and RAGNAR ROMMETVEIT

PILOT STUDIES OF ROTE LEARNING SITUATIONS

A series of five exploratory studies were conducted as preliminary preparation for an extension of the Louvain context study (Rommetveit *et al.*, 1971). In general since no evidence for a typical rote learning strategy was found in any of the experimental conditions in the Louvain study, an attempt was made at adding a more genuine rote learning experimental condition to the Louvain design.

In all experimental situations of the present series, the subjects (University students) were asked to learn the same set of eight Norwegian utterances. These utterances were constructed according to the same principles as those used in the Louvain experiment. Some improvements, however, were introduced: every sentence *ending* had two and only two content elements, and coupling of sentence beginnings and endings was pretested to check for transitional probabilities.

Although the learning procedure varies in the studies to be described, the subjects in all versions of the experiment were given the *same* recall tasks. Half of the subjects received a sentence completion recall task, whereas the other half received a content clue recall task. In general it was expected that subjects in the rote learning conditions would show a more accurate recall in a sentence completion recall task than subjects in non-rote learning conditions in which there was one presentation of the stimulus (cf. Louvain study). A more adventurous hypothesis would be that the former subjects would actually be *handicapped* when recall is prompted by a content clue. In comparison, a one-trial-learning, picture-context condition like the one in the Louvain study should thus yield better recall in the content clue recall situation than in sentence completion. These hypotheses are shown in Table 1. In what follows we

TABLE 1

Initial predictions

| | Recall performance | |
Condition	Content clue	Sentence completion
No context, five presentations	poor	good
Picture context, one presentation	good	poor

shall examine each of the successive versions of experimental conditions by which we tried to introduce a rote learning strategy. By doing so we shall try to explore which aspects of the learning situations are of particular significance for inducing a rote learning set toward meaningful verbal material. Our analysis will be based on the subjects' reported experience of the situation, as well as on observations of their recall under different prompting methods.

Study I

The first pilot study to be reported was an extension of the Louvain context study; a learning condition was added to the three main Louvain conditions (see pp. 109–125). Only geometrical figures (the *NC* figures from the Louvain study) were used as ready signals, and exposure time for ready signals was four seconds. During the first presentation, the sentence followed immediately after the slides. During the following four presentations the ready signal was presented eight seconds before the sentence was heard. During this eight-second interval the subjects were instructed to anticipate as exactly as possible the sentence that followed that particular figure. There were ten subjects in the learning condition, five in each of the two retrieval conditions.

Retrieval performance in both prompting conditions was, as far as a superficial comparison can be trusted, much better in the present study than in the study at Louvain, in which the sentences were presented only once. A strict comparison between the two studies is prohibited, however. Even though the stimulus material was very similar, we would have to make the comparison across two different languages. Moreover, the subjects in one case were Belgian soldiers and in the other Norwegian students.

Retrieval performance was much better when recall was prompted by a content clue than when prompted by the sentence beginning. Our hypothesis of good sentence completion and poor retrieval on the basis of content clue thus was clearly disconfirmed. This finding may possibly be explained as follows: the time for anticipating the sentences (eight seconds) may have been too long to yield a rote learning strategy; it may have been sufficient time to allow subjects to produce associations to the utterances as well as to make up connections between ready signal and utterance. Anticipation in the experimental situation described above thus was possibly a very active process, by which the utterances acquired additional "meaning". Some subjects, for instance, reported that they had even managed to establish meaningful relations between the geometrical figures and the utterances.

We had thus obviously established an experimental situation very different from a rote learning situation. And each of the four pilot studies reported below may be considered as successive steps in a search for a situation yielding an unequivocal medium-bound set toward meaningful verbal material.

Study IIa

In order to induce a more pure rote learning strategy, the experimenter presented each sentence orally to the subject, without any ready signal in advance. The subject was told to respond to each utterance with an immediate and complete repetition. Immediately after the subject had given his repetition, the experimenter presented the next sentence. Each of the eight sentences was presented and repeated five times; seven subjects went through this version of the learning experiment. Retrieval performance, however, again was much better in the content clue retrieval condition than in the sentence completion retrieval condition.

Study IIb

Except for presenting and repeating *each* sentence five times *before* presenting the next sentence, the experimental design was as described in IIa. Only six subjects participated in this pilot study.

Retrieval performance in this situation was very poor compared with the retrieval performance in the two situations mentioned above. More interesting, however, is the finding *that retrieval in this situation was as good when prompted by sentence beginning (sentence completion) as when prompted by content clues.*

Some of the subjects reported that after having been both presented and repeated four or five times the sentence became "meaningless", or, perhaps more adequately expressed, "empty of meaning". In this last version of the intended rote learning situation, it thus seems as if we may have come close to a condition of semantic satiation.

Study IIIa

This experiment was an attempt to standardize the last mentioned version (IIb) for further studies. The sentences were tape recorded. Five-second pauses were inserted between sentences. The subjects had been instructed to repeat the sentences during this time. Each utterance was thus presented and repeated five times before the next one was presented. Nine subjects took part in this study.

Recall, however, under these conditions was again better in the content clue retrieval condition than in the sentence completion retrieval condition. It was thought that the pause of five seconds might have been too long.

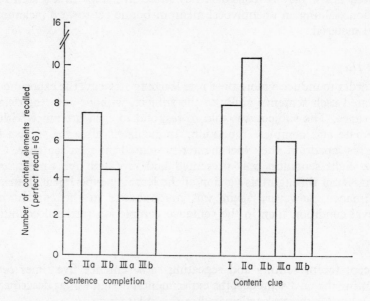

FIG. 1. Recall performance.

I: Anticipation of the sentences, geometrical figures used as ready signals. (Five presentations.)
IIa: Oral presentation and immediate repetition. (Five presentations followed by repetitions.)
IIb: Oral presentation and immediate repetition of the *same* sentence five times *before* the next sentence is presented.
IIIa: Tape-recorder-standardization of IIb, five seconds interval for repetition.
IIIb: Tape-recorder-standardization of IIb, three seconds interval for repetition.

Study IIIb

The experimental design was as described in IIIa, except that the pause between utterances was reduced to three seconds. Ten subjects went through this version.

Retrieval performance was now very poor, and about as good in the sentence completion retrieval condition as in the content clue retrieval condition.

All the results reported above are presented in Fig. 1. It shows average retrieval performance from all five learning situations described above, each column showing how many content elements of the sentence endings were given back. Perfect recall would give 16 (2 × 8) content elements. Only verbatim reproduction is included. Inclusion of synonyms would not change the pattern, however, since very few synonyms were given back.

Two tentative theoretical conclusions may be suggested at this stage:

(1) The fact that the sentence completion retrieval condition did not yield a better recall than the content clue retrieval condition in any of the intended rote learning situations indicates that subjects did not resort to extreme rote learning strategies of retrieval at all. It appears, therefore, *that it is very difficult indeed to induce experimental conditions in which a subject is forced to learn meaningful verbal material (as sentences) by using a rote strategy exclusively.*

(2) Retrieval performance is, of course, jointly determined by the learning situation and conditions of retrieval, such as whether recall is prompted by the beginning of the sentence or by some content clue that did not appear in the stimulus utterance at all. There is at the same time some evidence for an interaction effect. Content clues in most conditions seem to be more efficient prompts than sentence beginnings. This does not hold, however, for conditions which most genuinely seem to be experienced as rote learning situations (such situations as IIb and IIIb). The striking superiority of the content clue in the one-trial, picture-context condition of the Louvain experiment seems thus to break down in a many-trials rote learning condition.

FURTHER EXPLORATIONS OF LINKAGES BETWEEN CONTEXTS AND UTTERANCES

In the context study at Louvain, the linkage between the appropriate context and the utterance was supposed to be either one of implication or one of presupposition (see pp. 109–125). This distinction, however, is very complex and as yet not very thoroughly explored. In order to gain some more insight into such assumed subtle relationships between context events and utterances, the same set of eight pictures were used as appropriate contexts for two separate sets of eight utterances. For each picture, therefore, we constructed one utterance that was supposed to be linked to it by implication and another utterance representing a linkage of presupposition.

Consider, for example, the following two pictures from the Louvain study:

(1) *A drawing of a train leaving a station* (with small clouds of steam coming from the engine). The utterance linked to it by presupposition (Set I) is: "It's a pity she did not get there in time with the letter" (in Norwegian: "Det var trist at hun ikke kom tidsnok med brevet"). The implication (Set II) utterance for the same picture reads: "There were not enough concessions for electric power" (in Norwegian: "Det var ikke nok bevilgninger til elektrisk drift").

(2) *A drawing of a man knocking on a ceiling with a stick.* The utterance being linked to this picture context by implication (Set I) is: "The people above are continually making a noise" (in Norwegian: "Uavlatelig er det noen som lager støy ovenpå"). And the presupposition (Set II) utterance is: "Probably it will become quiet upstairs" (in Norwegian: "Antakeligvis blir det stille ovenpå").

These examples bring out two important and related aspects of the distinction between implication and presupposition. When the linkage is one of presupposition, the context event occurs *before* the event conveyed by the utterance (departure of train *before* late arrival; knocking on ceiling *before* quiet upstairs). When the utterance is linked by implication, on the other hand, it serves to explain some aspect of the visually presented context (old-fashioned steam engine *because of* lack of concessions; knocking on ceiling *because of* noise upstairs).

During and after the preparation of the second set of sentences, we tried to find out how naïve subjects spontaneously experienced these relationships. Each of the eight pictures was shown to naïve student subjects together with an oral presentation of the corresponding utterances. Each subject was asked to indicate, in a few words only, what relationship he perceived to exist between the picture and the utterance. The eight pictures were presented twice, first in connection with one, then in connection with the other of the two separate sets of sentences. This study was conducted as an informal discussion between the subject and experimenter, and only six students took part.

The assumed type of linkage seemed in most cases to be confirmed by the subject's spontaneous account of the connection between picture and utterance. When the linkage was one of implication, the subjects thus often actually spontaneously expressed the relationship perceived by means of a *"because"-statement*. This was never the case when the linkage was one of presupposition, and it seemed on the whole as if the latter linkage was somewhat more difficult to express in words.

Since each subject saw every picture twice, the first time in a presupposition linkage with an utterance and the second time in an implication linkage or vice versa, we were also in a position to explore possible sequence effects. More specifically, we were interested in finding out whether the first association of a given picture and an utterance affected the perceived linkage of that same picture with a second utterance.

No such sequence effect was observed when a presupposition linkage preceded an implication linkage, i.e. when *departing train–late arrival* preceded *departing train–lack of concessions for electric power*. The reverse sequence, on the other hand, brought out some interesting effects. Pictures that had first been experienced in a linkage of implication seemed to get attached to and somewhat "changed by" this first utterance, making it somewhat more difficult to cognize its connection to the second utterance. When presented with the picture the second time and then listening to the presupposition utterance, the subject occasionally claimed that "so and so" had already been told about that picture earlier. Sometimes he would even object that the new utterance appeared to be inconsistent with what had been said about that picture earlier. No evidence of such a "fixation" was observed, however, when a linkage of presupposition preceded one of implication. As expected, according to the initial analysis of the linkage of implication as involving *a retroactive process* some re-interpretation of the picture thus seemed to take place when it was followed by an implication utterance.

This hypothesized retroactive process will be further explored in a more carefully controlled study. Subjects will then simply be asked to describe every picture as exactly as possible. Exposure time will be four seconds, as in the context study, and three experimental conditions will be compared. One group of subjects will have only the pictures presented. Two other groups will have each picture immediately followed by an utterance as in the context study. One of these two groups will be given Set I of utterances, the other group will be given Set II. We shall thus be able to compare the descriptions of the same picture experienced in three different situations: in isolation, when linked to a presupposition utterance, and when linked to an utterance by implication.

This study will serve two different purposes. It will hopefully yield additional information about the stimulus material to be used in "the context and rote learning study" to be described below. In addition, it should shed some more light on the two types of context-utterance linkage as such.

A DESIGN FOR AN UTTERANCE-IN-CONTEXT VERSUS A ROTE LEARNING EXPERIMENT

As an extension of the Louvain study and on the basis of the pilot studies reported above, the following experiment is now being planned.

Utterances will be learned in one or the other of the following two main experimental situations.

(1) A more "natural" situation, namely, a "one-presentation picture-context situation" (cf. the picture-context condition in the Louvain study).

(2) In contrast to this, a situation assumed to induce a rote learning strategy, namely a "many-presentations, no-context situation" (cf. the IIIb situation described above).

Afterwards, half of the subjects in each of the two experimental situations will be given the sentence completion recall task, the other half will have the content clue recall task. The order of prompts, moreover, will be different for the two tasks: sentence completion retrieval will be in the same order as the initial sequence of presentation of utterances, whereas content clues will be given in a different order.

The stimulus material will consist of two separate sets of eight sentences (Sets I and II described above), constructed according to the same principles as before. To each of the eight pictures serving as appropriate contexts there will be one utterance linked to the picture by implication, and another utterance linked to it by presupposition. The same set of eight pictures is thus used in connection with the two different sets of utterances, and in such a way that a linkage of implication in Set I is replaced by presupposition in Set II, and vice versa. The complete design is presented in Table 2.

TABLE 2

Experimental design

	Contexts			
	None		Picture	
Set of utterances	Set I	Set II	Set I	Set II
Number of presentations	5*	5*	1	1
Retrieval conditions	CC SC	CC SC	CC SC	CC SC

CC = content clue
SC = sentence completion
* Five presentations and five repetitions.

What is intended is therefore a systematic comparison of two extreme conditions: a one-trial-learning of an utterance in a meaningful pictorial context versus a many-trials-learning of the same utterance under conditions approaching a rote learning (or semantic satiation) situation. The two prompting methods, moreover, differ markedly with respect to which level of processing is required for retrieval: with sentence beginnings as prompts *and* prompting sequence identical with sequence of presentation, a rote strategy of word-by-word and utterance-by-utterance sequential organization of the verbal material without any retention of higher-order message elements should suffice for successful retrieval. Such a strategy, however, should fail entirely when retrieval is prompted by content clues that did not appear in the stimulus utterance at all *and* when the order of such prompts differs from that of the order of utterances in the sequence of learning trials.

Our hope is that this experiment will help to illuminate further the difference between language processing in natural contexts and processing of the same verbal material under a medium bound set. If clearly different strategies are found to be operant in the two types of situations, it will emphasize that generalizing from typical laboratory learning studies to natural verbal communication is indeed hazardous.

A Method of Discourse Analysis Applied to Recall of Utterances

MICHEL PÊCHEUX

The present paper deals with a method of discourse analysis which has been presented elsewhere (Pêcheux, 1969) in a more general form. Here, the method will be applied to retrieval performance in an experimental study of context effects (Rommetveit *et al.*, 1971, pp. 29–56).

DESCRIPTION OF THE METHOD

The method to be briefly outlined below has been developed in order to explore mechanisms at a level between the level of language (meaning of the French word "langue") and the level of speech ("parole"). It aims at an analysis of what might be called "discourse structure". A discourse can be schematically depicted as shown in Fig. 1.

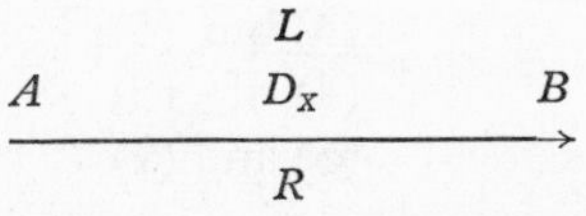

$$L$$
$$A \qquad D_X \qquad B$$
$$\overrightarrow{}$$
$$R$$

L = linguistic system; D_X = discursive string; A = the addresser; B = the addressee; and R = the referent or subject-matter of the discourse.

FIG. 1. Schematic representation of a discourse.

The structure of a discourse is assumed to be determined partly by a set of tacit production conditions. These production conditions represent the general social or interactional context in which the discourse takes place. The primary conditions include: (1) the representation that A has of himself in the discourse, $I_A(A)$; (2) the representation that A has of B in the discourse, $I_A(B)$; and (3) the representation that A has of R in the discourse, $I_A(R)$. In addition, there are "second order representations" such as $I_A(I_B(A))$, $I_A(I_B(B))$ and $I_A(I_B(R))$.

The method, when applied to a given sequence of discourse, therefore should allow for a systematic analysis of the relationship between specific

67

characteristics of the observed sequence of discourse (a discourse surface) and the production conditions under which the discourse is generated. Segments of discourse produced under identical production conditions (as far as subjective and situational criteria are concerned) constitute a corpus which can be analysed with respect to selection or paradigmatic sub-situation in a string of morphemes (for example: (I v you v he v this man), (drink v buy v like v demand v tell), (beer v wine v coffee v gin); operation a v b = "a or b, but not a and b") as well as combination or syntagmatic concatenation: ("I + drink + wine" or "he + like(s) + coffee").

Segments can then be decomposed into minimal utterances connected by binary relations. An utterance such as *"The flowers have too little light and heat"* can thus be decomposed into two minimal utterances connected by "and", i.e. into:

(1) *The flowers have too little light*
and
(2) *The flowers have too little heat.*

By this procedure, one obtains a list of minimal utterances. Each such minimal utterance contains a subject, a verb (possibly modified by an adverb), and possibly also a complement. Let $E = (1), (2) \ldots (n)$ be this list of minimal utterances.

At the same time, one obtains a list of binary relations between minimal utterances, B_x, such as, for instance:

$$B_x: \quad (1) \text{ and } (2)$$
$$(3) \text{ but } (4)$$
$$(4) \text{ if } (5)$$
$$(5) \text{ and } (7)$$
$$\cdot \quad \cdot \quad \cdot$$
$$\cdot \quad \cdot \quad \cdot$$
$$\cdot \quad \cdot \quad \cdot$$
$$\cdot \quad \cdot \quad \cdot$$

It is then possible to compare one pair of connected minimal utterances with some other pair that is combined by the same connector, and the outcome of such a comparison yields a measure of paradigmatic proximity between the two pairs. Table 1 shows the morphosyntactic categories used in assessing the proximity between two utterances represented in canonical form.

Consider two minimal utterances (with eight basic components each):

$$E_i = x_i^1, x_i^2, \ldots x_i^k, \ldots x_i^8 \text{ and}$$
$$E_j = x_j^1, x_j^2, \ldots x_j^k, \ldots x_j^8$$

When a Boolean vector is attributed to the pair $(E_i - E_j)$, a value of 1 is

TABLE 1

Canonical form of minimal utterances and proximity weighting

		F	D_1	N_1	V	ADV	PP	D_2	N_2
1	$X_1/X_1(X_1 \neq \phi)$	3	2	5	5	3	3	2	5
2	$X_1/X_1(X_1 = \phi)$	—	1	—	—	1	1	1	1
3	$X_1/X_1(X_1 = \epsilon)$	—	—	—	2	—	—	—	—

The 8 basic components of the canonical form used here are:

(1) F characterizing the form (including tense, modalities, aspect) of the utterance.

(2) D_1 determination of the subject (article, demonstrative etc. . . . .).

(3) N_1 subject of the minimal utterance.

(4) V verb: either a lexical term like *to be, to have, to buy* etc. or ϵ, characterizing the implicit copula (for instance: the great house; . . . →house ϵ great).

(5) ADV adverb.

(6) PP preposition introducing the complement (e.g. for, by etc. . . . .). When the complement is *directly* connected to the verb (case of "direct complement"), this connection is marked by "★".

(7) D_2 determination of the complement.

(8) N_2 complement of the verb in the minimal utterance.

The proximity weightings for each basic component are shown in line 1 when $x_i = \phi$ and ϵ; the weightings when $X_i = \phi$ or $X_i = \epsilon$ are shown in lines 2 and 3 respectively. Cells showing "—" are cases where no morphosyntactic co-occurrence is possible.

assigned if there is identity with respect to a given morphosyntactic category (when $x_i^k = x_j^k$, the kth proximity value will be 1), whereas 0 is assigned whenever different elements are observed (when $x_i^k \neq x_j^k$, the proximity value will be 0).

Each of these values is multiplied by a *weighting* which is attributed to each element of the Boolean vector, i.e. to each morphosyntactic category. If $x_i^k = x_j^k = \phi$ (this case can only occur for categories D_1, ADV, PP, D_2 and N_2, and refers to the instance in which the place of the considered category is empty[a]), then the weighting for each category will be equal to 1 (see line 2, Table 1). If $x_i^k = x_j^k = \epsilon$ (this case can only occur for category V and refers to an implicit copula, e.g. the great house . . . house ϵ great), then the weighting will be equal to 2 (see line 3, Table 1). For cases in which $x_i^k = x_j^k \neq \phi$ and $x_i^k = x_j^k \neq \epsilon$, the value of the proximity weighting is given in line 1 of Table 1. Cells showing a "—" in Table 1 are cases where no morphosyntactic co-occurrence is possible. A weighting, of course, implies an element of arbitrary decision; however, the basis on which these decisions were made will not be discussed here. The final measure of proximity is obtained by adding the weighted

[a] For instance: D_1 in "ϕ John walks often with his father". ADV in "the boy walks ϕ with his father, etc. . . . ."

instance of identity for each morphosyntactic category. For instance, if, in the pair $E_i - E_j$, identity occurred between elements in all the morphosyntactic categories shown in the canonical form of Table 1 and $x_i^k = x_j^k \neq \epsilon$ or ϕ (line 1, Table 1), the proximity between two minimal utterances would be:

$$(1 \times 3) + (1 \times 2) + (1 \times 5) + (1 \times 5) + (1 \times 3) + (1 \times 3) + \\ + (1 \times 2) + (1 \times 5) = 28.$$

As a specific example consider the following two complex utterances:

(A) *The flowers have too little light and heat.*

(B) *The plants have too little light and air.*

The components of utterance (A) are (1) and (2) as given above; the components of (B) are:

(3) *The plants have too little light.*

(4) *The plants have too little air.*

TABLE 2

Proximity assessment example

F	D_1	N_1	V	ADV	PP	D_2	N_2
F_x	The (plural)	flower	to have	too little	$\star$	(Indef. sing.)	light
F_x	The (plural)	plant	to have	too little	$\star$	(Indef. sing.)	light
1	1	0	1	1	1	1	1

The paradigmatic proximity between (1) and (3) can now be assessed by presenting each of the two minimal utterances in the canonical forms as shown in Table 2. When the proximity score is computed by summing the weighted scores for each morphosyntactic category, the comparison yields:

$$p(1, 3) = (1 \times 3) + (1 \times 2) + (0 \times 5) + (1 \times 5) + (1 \times 3) + \\ + (1 \times 3) + (1 \times 2) + (1 \times 5) = 23.$$

Thus the problem of paradigmatic proximity between apparently similar complex utterances is handled as an assessment of weighted *overlap* of corresponding components of the minimal utterances into which the complex utterances are analysed. By the same method we obtain $p(2, 4) = 18$ as the proximity between minimal utterances 2 and 4. The proximity between the complex utterances (A) and (B) above is then the sum of the proximity scores for (1, 3) and (2, 4), i.e. $23 + 18 = 41$.

AN APPLICATION OF THE METHOD TO RETRIEVAL OF UTTERANCES

In the study of context effects (Rommetveit *et al.*, 1971, pp. 29–56, this edition), complex utterances were presented to subjects under different experimental conditions. Retrieval performance was then scored in terms of correctly recalled content elements. Only the most intuitively salient content elements of the stimulus utterances were included in the retrieval measures, and no weighting of content elements was attempted.

The method of assessing paradigmatic proximity outlined above should yield a more sensitive measure of retrieval performance, and the method was therefore tried out for two of the stimulus utterances:

(Implication) "There was insufficient light and heat."

(Presupposition) "It's a shame she did not get there in time."

In one condition (Non-appropriate Context) these utterances were preceded by arbitrary geometrical figures (as signals for attention) and in another condition (Picture Context) by drawings of a fading flower and a train leaving a station, respectively. The linkages between a drawing of a context event and an utterance were supposed to be of two different kinds, a proactive *and* retroactive linkage of *implication* in the case of *flower/insufficiency of light and heat* and a unidirectional linkage of *presupposition* only in the case of *train/late arrival*. It was hypothesized, moreover, that a picture context would contribute more to message retrieval when the linkage between context and utterance was one of presupposition.

Performance Scoring of Content Elements

Table 3 gives the initial analysis (Louvain method) of retrieval performance for the two stimulus utterances in the Picture Context and Non-appropriate Context sub-conditions in which retrieval was prompted by a "content clue".

TABLE 3

Retrieval performance scoring of content elements

	Picture context	No context
Implication	10 (14)	8 (13)
Presupposition	6 (16)	1 (10)

Numbers in parentheses refer to total number of subjects responding; 20 subjects were in each experimental condition. Numbers to left show the number of subjects responding with at least *one* semantically correct content element.

The number in parenthesis shows how many of the 20 subjects in each group gave any response at all, whereas the number to the left in each cell is the number of subjects who gave back at least *one* semantically correct content element.

Two conclusions can safely be drawn from Table 3. There is, first of all, a fairly large number of subjects who have given back something without being able to "hit" any one of the salient content elements that were included in the initial recall measure. The pictorial context, moreover, apparently has more of a facilitative effect when the linkage is one of presupposition (6/1 versus 10/8), but the overall recall of the utterance "There was insufficient light and heat" is very poor. The number of subjects who gave back at least one correct content element item is actually too small for an X^2 analysis of the results.

Message Retrieval Scoring by Means of Paradigmatic Proximity Computation

First an attempt was made to compare every subject's reproduction of the utterance with the stimulus utterance. For example, consider the stimulus utterance "There was insufficient light and heat" and a hypothetical subject's reproduction "There was insufficient light and space". The stimulus sentence gives "There was insufficient light (and) there was insufficient heat"; the reproduction gives "There was insufficient light (and) there was insufficient space" (see Table 4).

Given the information in Table 4, the computation of the proximity between the example reproduction (there was insufficient light and space) and the stimulus utterance is then obtained by comparing the following subsets of minimal utterances (see Table 4):

ϕ_1		δ_2		δ_2	
(1),	(3)	(1),	(2)	(3),	(4)
(5),	(7)	(5),	(6)	(7),	(8)

The computation of the weighted proximity between minimal utterance pairs (1), (5) and (3), (7) is given in Table 5. The calculated proximity for these minimal utterance pairs as shown in Table 5 is $p(1, 5) + p(3, 7) = 25 + 20 = 45$. By this same method we obtain proximity values for the comparison of the other subsets of minimal utterances:

$$p(1, 5) + p(2, 6) = 25 + 21 = 46$$
$$p(3, 7) + p(4, 8) = 20 + 16 = 36$$

The values 45, 46, 36 rate step by step the proximity between the sequences A and B or more precisely, in the present case, the proximity between the stimulus utterance A and the subject's reproduction B.

But there is a problem here. If we consider now the response "There is dark and cold here", the comparison with the stimulus utterance leads

TABLE 4

Proximity comparison

A. *Stimulus Utterance*

E_x
(1) $F_2 \, \phi$	there be	ϕ	$*$	D_1	light
(2) $F_4 \, \phi$	light	$\epsilon \;\; \phi$	$*$	ϕ	insufficient
(3) $F_2 \, \phi$	there be	ϕ	$*$	D_1	heat
(4) $F_4 \, \phi$	heat	$\epsilon \;\; \phi$	$*$	ϕ	insufficient

B_x
(1) ϕ_1 (3)
(1) δ_2 (2)
(3) δ_2 (4)

$\phi_1 = $ and
$\delta_2 = $ determination of the complement in the left minimal utterances— (1) and (3)—by the right minimal utterances—(2) and (4).

$F_2 = $ indicative, preterite, active form.
$F_4 = $ intemporal relation, in connection with copula ϵ.
(1), (2), (3), (4) = set of minimal utterances "E_x".
(1) δ_2 (2) = example of binary relation, pertaining to set "B_x".

B. *Example Reproduction*

E_x
(5) $F_2 \, \phi$	there be	ϕ	$*$	D_1	light
(6) $F_4 \, \phi$	light	ϕ	$*$	ϕ	insufficient
(7) $F_2 \, \phi$	there be	ϕ	$*$	D_1	space
(8) $F_4 \, \phi$	space	ϕ	$*$	ϕ	insufficient

B_x
(5) ϕ_1 (7)
(5) δ_2 (6)
(7) δ_2 (8)

TABLE 5

Computation of proximity between minimal utterance pairs

Utterance pairs   (1) $F_2 \; \phi$ there be ϕ $*$ D_1 light   (3) $F_2 \; \phi$ there be ϕ $*$ D_1 heat
                  (5) $F_2 \; \phi$ there be ϕ $*$ D_1 light   (7) $F_2 \; \phi$ there be ϕ $*$ D_1 space

Identity value
assignment   1   1   1   1   1   1   1   1   1   1   1   1   1   1   1   0

Proximity values
(Identity values
$\times$ weightings) $3+1+5+5+1+3+2+5=25$ $3+1+5+5+1+3+2+0=20$

Proximity score $p(1, 5) + p(3, 7) = 25 + 20 = 45$

to a different and much smaller result. (This is because the semantic relationships between "insufficient light" and "dark" (for instance) are not taken into account. In other words, by this method we obtain a rote learning analysis, not a semantic comparison.

For this reason, we decided to consider *each group of reproductions as a corpus determined by a production condition, and to measure the paradigmatic proximities between all subjects' reproductions of the utterance, in each group.* In this way, it was possible to obtain a measure of the *semantic centration* of each group of responses, taking into account the semantic equivalences. We computed the *number of paradigmatic proximities which are higher than a given value* p, *called similitudes.* This number is given in Table 6 for each condition. When the X^2-test is applied to the data in this Table, the results show that the null-hypothesis can be rejected ($p < 0.001$). This contrast with the non-significant result of the X^2-test applied to the number of subjects who gave any response at all in each group (number in parenthesis, Table 3). This earlier finding means that the number of uttered responses in each group cannot be considered as a source of the difference shown in Table 6. The hypothesis concerning differential effects of a pictorial context, depending upon type of context-utterance linkage involved, is thus supported.

TABLE 6

Number of paradigmatic proximity scores higher than pα

	Picture context	Non-appropriate context
Implication	13	25
Presupposition	28	4

What constitutes a puzzle, however, is the fact that the utterance "There was insufficient light and heat" is recalled with greater semantic centration in the Non-appropriate Context condition than in the Picture Context condition when the method of paradigmatic proximity is used. A more detailed analysis shows that this is largely due to the fact that a lot of Non-appropriate Context-subjects gave back the word "insufficient". Thus in the Non-appropriate Context condition there are more cases of verbatim recall of one specific part of the utterance only, as is often the case in rote learning situations.

The method of discourse analysis illustrated above has as its primary purpose, as already mentioned, an assessment of some structural properties of connected discourse. The method has been developed into a computer program for automatic discourse analysis (Pêcheux, 1969). The present analysis, however, was carried out by hand. The outcome suggests that a measure of weighted paradigmatic proximity between pairs of utterances may also be useful as a means of measuring retrieval of complex verbal material.

Acknowledgement

We thank B. Provansal who kindly assisted us in this careful and detailed work.

REFERENCES

Pêcheux, M. (1969). "Analyse automatique du discours," Dunod, Paris.
Rommetveit, R., Cook, M., Havelka, N., Henry, P., Herkner, W., Pêcheux, M. and Peeters, G. (1971). Processing of utterances in context. *In* "Social Contexts of Messages" (E. A. Carswell and R. Rommetveit, eds), pp. 29–56. Academic Press, London and New York.

On Processing of Message Referents in Contexts*

PAUL HENRY

Most models of language processing involve an element, usually called a *referent*, which stands for the object or event about which something is being said. For instance, according to Jakobson (1960), any communication process involves at least six elements: a speaker, an addressee (or receiver), a linguistic code, a communication channel, a message, and a referent of the message. The referent is often considered to be the pivot of the relation between a message and the "extralinguistic reality". Therefore, the notion of referent would appear to be essential in the study of language in contexts. Unfortunately, this notion remains very imprecise and is, more or less, related to a conception of language in which words are thought of as labels applied to real or fictitious entities. The inherent difficulties of this conception of referent have been emphasized for some time; however, there is still room for an elaboration of the referent conception which would be more appropriate to the empirical and theoretical study of the various aspects of communication processes.

In this paper we will suggest a conception of referent which may be useful to the study of some aspects of communication processes, in particular to the study of ideological processes. The present conception is rooted in a theoretical analysis of communication processes which implies that the relationships (1) between a message and the language, and (2) between a message and contexts, involve other messages or discourses *not involved* in the contexts in the usual sense. The functioning of a message in relation to other messages in production or interpretation will be called a *discursive process* (other concepts like *conditions of production of discourses, representations, tied and free information, generator of a discourse*, etc., will be introduced later).

* A previous version of this paper has been discussed to great extent with Professor Ragnar Rommetveit who has also done substantive editorial work on it. The present paper is the product of these discussions and editorial work.

Now the notion of context will be analysed so that it will be possible to differentiate among the various relations between a message and the communication it covers. A general model of message production and interpretation will be sketched and some directions for experimental investigation will be suggested.

REFERENTS, MESSAGES AND DISCOURSES

Wiener and Mehrabian (1968) tell us that when a mother calls (1) "Johnny, come home", her son is less likely to return quickly than if she commands (2) "Johnny, come home!", or (3) "John James Smith, come home". Different explanations of this fact and of similar ones can be postulated. However, at present we will concern ourselves with sentence wording and not with other factors like variation in the intensity of the voice which may also command the attention of the addressee (e.g. the command intonation in sentence 2).

Regarding sentence (3) it can first be said that this wording is unusual in a situation involving a mother and her child, and as a result Johnny would be surprised and feel threatened. It seems to combine sentence (1) with *stylistic modulations* stressing the imperative character of the mother's call. In other words, it can be said that the two utterances have the same *denotative meaning* whereas, in sentence (3), the wording adds a *connotative component of meaning* indicating a threat. Following Wiener and Mehrabian (1968), we can apply the notion of *immediacy*, that is, the notion of "relationship between the speaker and the objects about which he communicates, the addressee of his communication and the communication itself". The registry office names used in sentence (3) are called an indicator of non-immediacy, or an indicator of "a separation of the speaker from the objects he communicates about, the addressee or the communication itself". When using sentence (3), the mother seems to stand more aloof from her child than when using sentence (1); the expected result then would be that the child would feel this separation, find it unbearable, and as a result would be obliged to obey.

In spite of what is said about the possible impact of surprise and threat and about mother-child relationships, these interpretations of the differences between sentences (1) and (3) nevertheless remain *ad hoc* and their generalization would encounter severe difficulties. Among other things, it would be necessary to define a set of criteria in order to decide which linguistic form is a neutral or usual one (i.e. not carrying specific connotations or indicators of non-immediacy) and which linguistic form is an interpretable variation.

The relationship between these two utterances is difficult to grasp if one does not take into account the background information, namely why there are two different forms, why the mother can use either of the forms depending on the situation, and why the boy is able to interpret the forms differently. The first contact a child has with his registry office names usually occurs when he goes to school. This is not so just by chance; registry office names are tied to the existence of an institution, the family, and to the fact that other institutions than the family exist. So, registry office names in general *refer* people to their families; when used at school, they *refer* pupils to their family. If the boy, however, has never been called by his registry office names or if he has not heard or seen them used in rather official circumstances by people vested with institutional authority, it is possible to hypothesize that sentence (3) would not differ in impact from sentence (1). On the other hand, as a name like "Johnny" is the name used at home, any contrast with this name might be effective anyway.

It could be said, then, that the relationship between sentence (1) and sentence (3) is relative to specific cultural backgrounds. If we analyse this example more closely, it is possible to go beyond specific cultural factors to a more general account of such facts. What happens when registry office names are used by one member of the family speaking to another member of the family? It is evident that this does not *refer* the addressee, or the person communicated about, to the family. The only possible interpretation is that there is an *apparent shifting* of the speaker's locus outside the family. In our example, the mother has a locus in the family and the child has another place in it. At the same time, the mother has a locus relative to the school institution (being the mother of a pupil) and the child has another locus within the same institution. In school other loci are connected to these, those of the headmaster, of the teachers, of other pupils, etc. When the mother says "John James Smith, come home", her locus in the family has apparently shifted to the locus of the school headmaster. The shifting is *apparent*, because it is relative to a message or a discourse, i.e. the mother does not really immediately become a school director. When she speaks to her boy, what is dominant is that they are both in the *family*. So, the mother occupies two different loci at the same time, her real locus in the family and an apparent one which could be called her *position*. As defined here, the *position* is always related to messages, discourses or behaviours, whereas the *locus* is determined by the social structure.

What was called non-immediacy or connotative meaning earlier, has now been related to an apparent shifting of the speaker from one locus to another. This process of shifting implies that there is, at one and the same time, an invariant in the relationship between the speaker and the addressee (here, their relative loci in the family) and apparent changes. It is not the fact that the boy is called "John James Smith" which is important, but that it is his mother who calls him so. This explains why we do not consider that registry office names are intrinsically indicators of non-immediacy. Another important point is that the locus corresponding to the position the mother takes is connected to the boy's locus in the school. This is why the boy can interpret the shift. If the child is very young, there is nothing outside his family. Then, by itself (i.e. not accompanied by specific prosodic features in the mother's voice, which have already accompanied a threat followed by action) the usage of registry office names would be meaningless and the reactions of the child would be unpredictable.

As the process of shifting and the constraints to which it is submitted are very important from our point of view, it is necessary to discuss it in greater detail. An important idea which must be introduced is that, given the locus a person occupies in the social structure and given the situation in which he is embedded, he cannot adopt the discourse and conduct of every other possible locus. More precisely, the position he assumes when he apparently shifts toward another locus depends not only upon *that locus* but also upon *his own locus*. It is evident that everybody cannot behave in every possible way or say everything possible. These constraints are usually considered to be related to cultural or social norms (see the notion of *boundary conditions*, introduced by Wiener and Mehrabian, 1968). But in addition to the idea of norms there is the idea of transgression. If every kind of limit or constraint which specifies the particular form and interpretation of a communication were a social or cultural norm, it could always be transgressed although this might seldom occur. When we say that it is not possible to assume every possible locus, we refer to a much stronger constraint.

In order to substantiate this idea which contradicts prevailing ones, we will use two kinds of illustration. First there is the study of conflict situations by Plon (1969). In this work, subjects were asked to imagine themselves, for instance, as the leader of a trade union confronted with the manager of a factory and having to make a decision to launch a strike or not. The results were that subjects belonging to lower classes gave outcomes which clearly differed from those given by subjects belonging to higher classes; in contrast, when the same subjects were asked to imagine themselves as a patient confronted with a physician, there was no difference between the two populations. When subjects were not asked to imagine themselves in the locus of a trade union leader or a patient confronted with an employer or a physician respectively, but were asked to guess what would be the *decision* of the trade union leader or of the patient in the same respective situations, the differences also disappeared. The results of the study suggest that the positions the two categories of subjects assume when required to imagine themselves as a leader of a trade union facing a manager are different; in contrast, there is no significant difference between the positions each category of subjects assumes when required to imagine themselves as a patient confronted with a physician.

Plon's (1969) analysis of decision making in a conflict situation can be extended to message production and interpretation. One could, for instance, ask people belonging to different social classes to summarize texts having a clear ideological connotation and ask other people belonging to the same social class to perform the same task while imagining themselves as belonging to a class differing from their own.

The foregoing analysis has to do with the influence of so-called sociological or economic factors only and has therefore, it may be argued, nothing to do with our previous example of the mother and child. However, they are related. First, ideological factors are always tied to sociological and economic factors. Second, the existence of family and school as institutions is also tied to economic factors. Third, we encounter similar kinds of constraining limitations in one other field at least—the psychoanalytic investigation of discourse and behaviour. Freud has clearly shown, and other investigators in the same area confirm, that what we do and what we say, even the words we use, are highly dependent upon factors which are out of our conscious control. And in a given situation, at a given moment, there are utterances and discourses that a person cannot produce even if he has the required competence.

Now, what we suggest is that economic, institutional and ideological factors are intimately tied to a locus occupied by an individual in the social structure. These factors constitute the conditions of production of the individual's discourses and the conditions of interpretation of those he receives. Through these conditions of production, the range and types of positions a given individual can adopt are determined. In order to go further, we will borrow an example from C. Herzlich (1969). When studying the relationship between patients and physicians in health institutions in France, she noticed that physicians referred to their patients either as "this patient" or as "my patient". In France, most patients are admitted to a hospital through the out-patient clinic. They do not belong to the private practice of any physician of the hospital. Usually these patients are lower- or middle-class people. On the other hand, a physician working in a hospital but also having a private practice sends private patients to the hospital. These private patients are treated in the physician's department or in the department of one of his colleagues. The latter usually belong to upper classes. The two categories of patients do not belong to the same social class, they do not have the same institutional status in the hospital. Ordinary patients do not pay for medical care while private patients do. Each category of patient is treated in a separate ward.

Herzlich noticed that physicians used the term "this patient" selectively for the first category of patients, whereas they used "my patient" for private patients only. There is just one notable exception to this rule; a patient having an illness which is medically interesting, an illness about which the physician may write a publishable "*étude de cas*", is called "my patient" even if he is a non-private patient. At the same time, the attitude towards the patient is modified; the physician becomes interested in his patient's job, family, hobbies, etc. This does not occur with "these patients" who are treated impersonally, the illness being the primary consideration. But the publication of an "*étude de cas*" is one of the customary ways of acquiring a reputation as a physician. It must also be noted that the kind of physicians who have a private practice and a hospital job at the same time, are either professors in the medical faculty or are working to become professors. To a great extent, the reputation of a private physician and the amount of money he can ask for a consultation are dependent directly upon whether he is a member of the faculty and is on the hospital staff.

In this case, economic, institutional, and ideological factors (concerning medical practice and medical science, in particular) are clearly interwoven. The two possible loci of patients in the hospital are related through the physician's own loci. The physician apparently has two different loci as a physician, one in the hospital and one outside in his private practice, and these two connected loci interact. It is also possible to say that there is just one locus and that, among the economic, institutional and ideological factors which are tied to it, some elements only become dominant in a given situation, depending on the locus of the addressee or of the person communicated about. Loci are not intrinsically defined, but rather are defined in relation to other loci. When the physician calls an ordinary patient who has an interesting illness, "my patient", elements which are not usually dominant with ordinary patients become dominant. Such an analysis might also be applied to the mother and the child; instead of saying that the mother has a locus in the family and another in the school, it can be said that some elements tied to the locus of the mother become dominant in the family institution and others become dominant in the school institution. The apparent shifting, then, is related to a change with respect to dominance of the various factors.

Now we can give a better definition of the concept of *conditions of production* (and *interpretation of messages*). What are termed conditions of production are the complete set of economic, institutional, and ideological factors tied to a given locus and involved in message production and interpretation. In a given situation, only some of the factors constituting the conditions of production are relevant and involved in the processes. Thus, we will have to consider different *states of the conditions of production.*[a] Conditions of production are tied to a locus determined by economic, institutional, and ideological factors whereas a state of the conditions of production is embedded in a situation and is relative to an individual who occupies a given locus within the social structure. The state of the conditions of production is dependent upon the connections between the locus of the speaker and the locus of the addressee, as well as upon the environment.

Now, let us summarize what we have advanced. Conditions of production and interpretation of the discourses are tied to the different loci assigned to people by social structures. In a given situation, only some elements of these conditions are dominant, and the latter make up a state of the conditions of production. In messages or discourses, people take positions according to the state of their conditions of production. From the point of view of the receiver, these positions may appear as an apparent shift of the locus of the speaker. This explains why messages may appear at first glance to be surprising or unusual, as indicators of non-immediacy, or as carrying connotative meaning.

It remains to identify what indicates apparent shiftings of this kind in messages or discourses. This brings us back to a discussion of referents, or at least, to the conception of referents we suggest. What we call *referent is considered to be constructed in discourses which are tied to specific conditions of production.* For instance, the referent associated with "Johnny" is constructed in messages occurring in the family whenever the boy is spoken to or about. Similarly, the referent associated with "John James Smith" is constructed in discourses or messages occurring in institutions outside the family. More precisely, the referents are constructed in discourses corresponding to a state of the conditions of production in which the relevant elements are those associated with the institution in which they occur. When the mother speaks to her boy, the relevant elements in the conditions of production of her messages are tied to her relationship with her child in the family. In this case "Johnny" is used to call the boy. Conversely, when "John James Smith" is used,

---

[a] For more details concerning the concept of conditions of production see Pêcheux (1969).

the relevant elements pertain to an institution outside the family. When the mother says "'John James Smith", elements in her conditions of production which are not tied to the family but which stem from the idea of an institutional, lawful authority, become dominant. It is because "Johnny" appears tied to discourses or messages used within the family and because "John James Smith" appears tied to discourses or messages occurring outside the family that an apparent shift takes place. When the mother calls "John James Smith", her message functions in connection with discourses and messages which occur outside the family; when the mother calls "Johnny", her message functions in connection with messages which occur within the family. The speaker thus takes different positions according to the discourses in which the actual message is functioning.

It is now necessary to analyse how messages or discourses function in connection with other discourses and messages, how referents are constructed in messages, etc. This is the purpose of the following section. However, in order to do this, we will have to take into account language and the way it functions.[b] We must take this occasion to stress the difference between the linguistic approach to language and our own approach. The study of discursive processes, of discourses functioning in connection with other discourses, implies that we work with a corpus of messages and that we take into account the loci of speakers and addressees. Modern linguists tend to work more with permissible sentence types and not so much with a corpus of utterances; they choose examples in order to make salient the similarities and differences within one language or between languages. They do not, as a rule, take into account the conditions of production or the loci to which messages are tied. It is possible for a linguist to work out a grammar covering all possible sentences in a language. A given speaker may still not be able to produce each and every

---

[b] By functions of the language we refer to, for instance, the concept of grammar developed by Chomsky. As a theory of the sentences of a language, a grammar is a theory of the functions of a language. It tells us, for instance, that when applying a passive transformation to

The dog has heard the thief

we get

The thief has been heard by the dog

whereas the passive transformation cannot be applied in a similar way to

The dog has heard the thief entering

The grammar, by means of an analysis of structural constituents, explains why the transformation can be applied in the first case and not in the second. Later we will have to refer to the linguistic theories developed by Culioli (1968) which form a bridge between linguistics and theory of discourse.

one of these sentences, however, even if he has the competence or potential to do so. Although the approaches of linguists and social psychologists differ, they are not mutually exclusive (see Moscovici, 1967).

TIED AND FREE INFORMATION REFERENTS AND ASSERTION

In his study of the relationships between code and messages, Jakobson (1957) has pointed to the fact that other messages and even the code can work in connection with messages. Here we will introduce a distinction between the free and the tied information carried by a message. This distinction is related to the notion of shifter used by Jakobson and to Frege's logical analysis of some syntactic patterns (Frege, 1892).[c]

Let us consider the sentence, "Unfortunately she arrived". We can say that, in this sentence, "she arrived" carries free information, whereas "unfortunately" carries tied information. The information carried by "she" (versus "he", for instance), by "arrived" (versus "left"), by "she arrived" (versus "she does not arrive", "she arrives", "she did not arrive", etc.) is not dependent upon any other element of the sentence. On the contrary, the information carried by "unfortunately" (versus "fortunately", for instance) is dependent upon the rest of the sentence. This is because "unfortunately" can be introduced only when the choices have been made between the different possible forms which could be used in place of "she arrived". More intuitively, we could have said that one cannot say that something is "fortunate" or "unfortunate" until what is to be declared so is determined.

This type of logical relationship between different parts of a sentence appears in many different forms in language. First, "unfortunately" (or "it is unfortunate that . . .") functions in the sentence in a way similar to what logicians call modalities. Instead of "unfortunately", we could have had "certainly" or "probably", etc. Second a similar situation appears with what is called *determination*. Let us take the sentence *"Atoms whose d-shell is not saturated are fissible"*. The relative proposition, "whose d-shell is not saturated", determines a sub-category of atoms, namely the category of atoms having a non-saturated d-shell. If we do not assume that it is possible to characterize a sub-category of atoms unequivocally by saying that they have "a non-saturated d-shell", the whole sentence is meaningless. On the other hand, if we do not assume that "fissible" may refer to an attribute of atoms, the whole sentence does *not* become meaningless; we can still infer from it that atoms having

---

[c] See also the theory of names and description in symbolic logic in Reichenbach (1947).

a non-saturated d-shell exist. We can hence say that the two parts of the sentence do not have the same logical status: "whose d-shell is not saturated" carries free information whereas "are fissible" carries tied information.[d] Given the connection between adjectives and relative propositions, we get a similar case with, for instance, "Dense numbers are integers" "dense" carries free information whereas "are integers" carries tied information.

These examples clearly show that the distinction between free and tied information is closely related to specific linguistic features of sentences—modalities, determination, etc. It is on the basis of a linguistic analysis that we can detect other linguistic features related to this distinction. The principles of such a linguistic analysis have been set up by Culioli (1968) who provides the basis for an analysis of sentences in what he calls a *lexis*. A lexis consists of a predicate and two classes of argument. For instance, in "the boy opens the door", we have one lexis— "boy", "door", "to open". In order to obtain the above sentence, different things must be tied to the lexis. Among other things, the classes of argument must be so determined that we get "the" instead of "a", or "this", or "one", etc.; the predicate must be also so determined that we get "opens" instead of "opened", "has opened", will open" or other forms.

The theory is much more complex than this brief outline suggests, but it is impossible to go into it in detail here. What is interesting to us, however, is that the lexis is *pre-assertive*, whereas everything that is added to the lexis pertains to *assertion* itself. By "assertion", Culioli means "assertion by a subject"; more specifically, everything that is added to lexis in order to determine elements within them or in order to combine them implies relations between the speaker and other persons. When I say "the boy . . .", I must be speaking of a well-specified person and I infer that I am giving sufficient cues to the addressee to identify him. The distinction between free and tied information is thus relative to assertion and not just to the set of lexis which are used to build up the utterances. It is the specific arrangement of lexis and the specific determination of elements within them which introduce the distinction: *tied information is relative to an assertion about an assertion.* So, we can say that "unfortunately" is an assertion about the assertion "she arrived", that "are fissible" is an assertion about the assertion "there are atoms whose d-shell is not saturated."

Then, if the distinction between free and tied information is relative

---

[d] Notice that what corresponds to "she arrives" in the first example is "whose d-shell is not saturated", and in the second what corresponds to "unfortunately" is "are fissible".

to assertion, it must imply relations between the speaker and other persons. In order to clarify this and in order to establish a connection between this logical-linguistic analysis and the foregoing section, we will use an example pertaining to political events. In a speech addressed to the American Congress before a vote on an increase of income taxes, President Johnson said something like: "It is not the regular increase of the administration charges that calls for an increase of income taxes but the Vietnam war".[e] In this utterance, "that calls for an increase of income taxes" is free information; "It is not the regular increase of the administration charges . . . but the Vietnam war" is tied information. What strikes us in this example is that it was said before the vote. The utterance relies on the assumption that income taxes *must* be increased, otherwise it would not be worth discussing whether it is the increase of administration charges or the Vietnam war which called for that increase of taxes. In a way there is a complete reversal of the logical order of arguments. Instead of demonstrating that income taxes must be increased, President Johnson apparently starts with the assumption that they must be increased anyway and then centres the discussion on factors necessitating this increase.

In order to give a full account of this example, we would have to refer to many different factors like the specific features of the political institutions of the United States, the history of the relationships between the Executive and the Congress, the political situation of the moment, etc. This would lead us too far away from our purpose. Let us just notice that, from a logical point of view, it is not possible to discuss what calls for an increase of taxes, if it is not assumed that something really calls for such an increase. The sentence is constructed in such a way that the increase of taxes is presented as a factual necessity requiring an explanation which is suggested in the part of the sentence carrying tied information.   Now, at the moment, for political, economic, and ideological reasons, there was an almost general agreement concerning the Vietnam war, whereas, at the same time, for reasons peculiar to local politics, some congressmen were hostile to an increase of taxes.   This conflict appears in the speech of the President seen from his own point of view as Chief of the Executive. The sentence is built up in such a way that the tied information it conveys (Vietnam war) induces the addressees to agree upon the free information (increase of taxes) to which this information is tied. In order to accept and interpret this sentence as a production of their own, the congressmen would have to make an apparent shift from their own locus (persons elected by local institutions) to the locus of the

---

[e] This quote is taken from a French translation which appeared in newspapers.

speaker. It will be recalled that this kind of shifting is not always possible, that it is constrained and limited by factors tied to loci in social structures. We can now analyse the conditions under which such messages can achieve their goal.

When a sentence can be analysed into two parts, one carrying free information and one carrying tied information, it may seem natural that the free information works as a basis on which speakers and addressees agree, whereas the tied information expresses the opinion, explicit assumptions, judgments, etc. of the speaker. However, it frequently happens that implicit assumptions are more important in the communication processes than explicit ones. In particular, when the implicit assumptions imply an apparent shift of the locus of the addressees. This often occurs in political and ideological discourses, but is not restricted to such types of discourse.

When we say to persons to whom the mathematical concept of integer is at least roughly known, "The dense numbers are integers", we induce these persons to think that the concept of dense number is constructed in the discourse of mathematics. If our assumptions are valid, the same process should be less likely to occur when it is said that "the integers are dense numbers". In this latter case, the part of the sentence carrying tied information contains the unknown notion.[f]

The above assumptions may be explored experimentally. We can for instance construct a sequence of sentences that can be divided into four subgroups:

1. Sentences which do not contain any concept, notion, or property unknown to pupils of a secondary school.
2. Sentences in which only the part carrying free information contains unknown notions or concepts.
3. Sentences in which only the part carrying tied information contains unknown notions or concepts.
4. Sentences in which both parts contain unknown notions or concepts.

The pupils would have to decide whether, according to them, each sentence is a scientific statement or not. A scientific statement could be operationally defined as a quotation from a scientific textbook. Sentences belonging to Groups 1 and 4 would act as control and we would expect the pupils to accept sentences within Group 2 more readily as scientific statements than would be the case for sentences within Group 3.

---

[f] See Moscovici (1967). The work of the axiomatic school in mathematics may be considered as an attempt to reduce to a set of primitive concepts the free information occurring in the discourse of mathematics.

Such an experimental setting deals only with particular aspects of the process, namely those related to the dichotomy of tied information/free information. It does not vary the positions of the speaker and of the addressee. If the sentence "Dense numbers are integers" is spoken by a teacher to pupils, the latter would more likely associate some meaning to dense number than if the sentence were spoken by another pupil. The reason is that a teacher by virtue of his locus in an educational institution is a person who tells scientific truths. If, on the other hand, the speaker were a pupil, there would be an apparent shifting of the speaker's locus. When a pupil embeds unknown concepts in his assertion as basic elements, he apparently adopts the locus of the teacher in the eyes of the other pupils. This hypothesis can also be tested. A second group of pupils can simply be asked to decide whether or not the sentences are quotations from texts produced by other pupils at their same level. The experimental situation is then the same as for the first experimental group of subjects, except for a change in the locus of the potential producer of the sentences; we now have a pupil as author instead of a scientific textbook. It is hypothesized that no significant difference with respect to acceptance of scientific statements will be found between the sentences from the first and fourth subgroups in either experimental group of subjects. On the other hand, significant differences should be found in response to sentences of the second and third type; the frequency of acceptance as scientific statements for both types of sentence should be inferior for the second experimental group of subjects. Moreover, the significant difference between sentence types two and three in the first experimental group should disappear in the second experiment when the pupils assume that the sentences have been produced by other pupils. The question is not whether pupils can identify wrong statements, but how sentences with elements not known as pertaining to scientific theories are interpreted in different ways depending upon the loci at which they are assumed to be produced.

We shall now return to the study of the relationships between the free information in messages and conditions of production. Sentences within Groups 2 and 3 involve elements which can be related to previous knowledge, given the conditions of production of the experimental subjects. The subjects have an idea of what a "number" is and of what something "dense" is. The problem is that they cannot easily imagine how the association between these two more or less empirical notions can work as a concept in mathematical discourse. In a sense the problem is one of shifting from empirical knowledge to scientific knowledge. On the other hand, when they are induced to give a meaning to "dense number", this meaning is dependent upon their previous empirical notions of numbers and what something "dense" is. The contrast between the case in which only the free information in the message involves unknown concepts and the case in which tied information involves it, results from these distinctly different origins of the two types of information. Free information refers to other discourses or messages (in the present case, to scientific discourses) whereas the tied information appears to be constructed in the actual message itself and thus does not implicitly involve other messages. Two types of factors will hence interact in the construction of referents. One factor is the relationship between the loci of speakers and addressees; the second factor has to do with the relationship between free and tied information within a given message. These two factors are closely related, since free information refers to discourses which are tied to different loci and positions.

This analysis may help us to understand transformation of scientific theories through vulgarization, as well as the formation of ideological notions (see Moscovici, 1961). Such processes involve not only the messages in which ideological and scientific notions occur, but also the conditions of production of producers and addressees. This brings us back to the study of the relationship between the free information in messages and the conditions of production. In order to deal with this problem, it is helpful to introduce what we call *representations*. The representation underlying a message refers to the assumptions which provide the basis *for the free information* carried by that message. When one says, "the man who walks in the street has lost his hat", it is implicitly assumed that there is actually one man walking in the street. This assumption is a prerequisite for transmission of information. In this sense, the representation could be identified with the message topic, i.e. the events (real, assumed, or imagined), the situations, the states of affairs, etc., about which something is said in the message. The free information is a basis for the empirical identification of these events, states of affairs, etc. In the present case, the representation would involve one man walking in a street, a person about which something is said in the message. But it is possible to analyse real, assumed, or imagined events, states of affairs, etc., in many different ways. Instead of "*the man who walks in the street*", one could have said "*the man with a red shirt*". Thus, it is necessary to differentiate between the empirical object which can be associated to a message and the way it is presented in the message. The difference becomes very important when political, ideological or scientific positions are involved. Fundamentally, this representation can be defined in terms of a set of relations between notions. For instance, with our last example we would have ("man", "street", "to walk") instead of ("man", "shirt", "has") or ("shirt", "red", "is"). It is helpful to identify the representation underlying a message with the set of lexis which are necessary to build up the part of the sentence carrying free information. These lexis are embedded in the terminal linguistic sequence and they function in it as a basis for determination or as something to which modalities are connected. The breakdown of a sentence into the lexis it contains and the analysis of the connections between these lexis provide a basis for the determination of the representation underlying that sentence. When we consider a single isolated sentence, the representation underlying that sentence must be connected to the part of the message carrying free information. The representation depends upon the way in which and in what part of the sentence the lexis are embedded. Thus, representations are connected to the process of assertion by a speaker. If we turn to a sequence of sentences, we must speak of a process of representation underlying the *sequence*, because the free information appearing in one sentence can be tied to a previous sentence (see Moscovici, 1961). In this sense, relations between notions that are introduced when tied information is connected to the free information can be incorporated into the representation underlying the sequence. Such a process may explain the conditions under which a text appears as a whole rather than as a set of disconnected sentences (see Bellert, 1968).

If it is recalled that determination and modalities imply relations between subjects, between the speaker and the message, etc., the advantages of our definition of representation become clear. In a way, the representation, being one step in the process of message production, appears as the basis on which a position is taken in the message and the basis on which something is constructed in the message.

Differences between representations indicate differences in the analysis of the real, assumed, or imagined events, situations, states of affairs which the message is about, as well as differences in the positions of the speakers. They can also indicate differences in the loci occupied by different speakers within the social structure and hence also differences in their economic, political, and ideological positions. The different representations a speaker uses in his messages would correspond to the different states of his conditions of production.

We now turn to the decoding processes. We must then assume that in order to interpret the messages he receives, the addressee must elaborate representations in connection with those messages. If the addressee is not able to build up such representations, the message is meaningless for him. The conditions under which he is able to elaborate such representations are also dependent upon the state of his conditions of production.

We can now sketch a theoretical model of message production and interpretation. Let us call Γ the conditions of production tied to a given locus in the social structure. Then Γ_i will represent the state of these conditions of production at a given stage of the process in a given situation. R_i is the representation built on the basis of Γ_i and forms, as such, the basis for the message. The set of lexis contained in R_i are connected to modalities and to other notions and lexis to form what is called the generator (Δ) of the message. Finally, the terminal linguistic sequence is produced through a stylistic modification (prosodic features and permutations of the order of elements). The process of production can be schematically represented by the following diagram:

$$\Gamma_i \longrightarrow R_i \longrightarrow \Delta_i$$

Now we turn to the production of *a sequence* of assertions. Here we must take into account the process by which the relations, introduced in the terminal sequence when tied and free information are connected together, are incorporated into the representation. The differences between R_i and Δ_i are analysed through an internal decoding process. This process implies a change in the state of the conditions of production and the elaboration of a new representation R_{i+1} in which the new relations are incorporated. Then the generator Δ_{i+1} is constructed on the basis of R_{i+1}

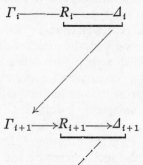

The external decoding process (the decoding of messages by the addressee) involves the construction of representation R_i' in connection with the received messages. This representation is also based on the state of the conditions of production Γ_i' of the addressee:

$$\Delta_i \qquad R_i' \longleftarrow \Gamma_i'$$

The differences between R_i' and Δ_i are then analysed. One outcome is a change in the state of the conditions of production of the addressee. It is on the basis of this new state of conditions of production that the representation underlying his answer will be elaborated:

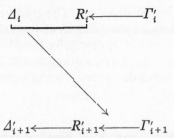

Thus, assuming that the changes in the state of the conditons of production are due only to the message exchanged and not to a modification of the environment, a process of representation between two persons can be represented in the figure below.

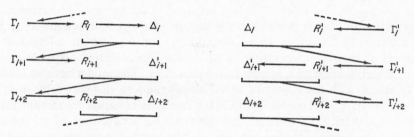

Encoding and decoding processes in a communication process.

This model is very similar to a model which was developed by Pêcheux (1969) as a theoretical basis for the development of an automatic discourse analysis. It differs only in the introduction of representational processes underlying message production and interpretation. It enables us to differentiate between the empirical objects which can be associated with a message and the referents which are constructed in messages and discourses (see Rommetveit, 1968). The construction of such referents involves the conditions of production of discourse and the locus in the social structure to which these conditions of production are tied. Referents are connected to discourses, and not to the language. In this sense, there is no referent for the word "table", for instance; referents are relative to discourses produced and interpreted in given conditions. This holds for words like democracy, capitalism, socialism, liberty, etc., as well as for scientific concepts. A scientific concept is associated with a word having a regulated function in discourses produced under conditions which enable the production of scientific theories; an ideological notion is associated with words which function in specific ways in discourses tied to specific loci in the social structure. The study of the representations underlying discourses and messages and of the function of notions and concepts inherent in them (i.e. of discursive functions as well as the study of the relationships between representations and conditions of production) may help us to understand the corresponding aspects of communication processes.

CONCLUSION AND PERSPECTIVES

In studies of language processing, words such as context, situation, referent, etc., have tended to confound factors which influence this process in very different ways. In order to clarify these issues, we have elaborated a complex model of language processing which should enable us to separate the different factors involved in the process. The essential contribution of this model is a distinction between representations and generators of discourse. This distinction has been related to a linguistic model of language processing in which the representations appear at a pre-assertive level with respect to the generator. The model has also been connected with the theory of social representations developed by social psychologists (Moscovici, 1961). This model is assumed to account for the contribution of internal decoding to the progression of complex discourse as well as for the connections between the messages exchanged in a communication process. It also serves to account for the construction of ideological notions through a communication process.

We have to distinguish between three types of effect exerted on discourse by context. The first is what could be called a *social effect* ("*effet de société*") exerted at the level of the conditions of production of messages through the interdependence of the loci of individuals in a social structure. The second type is a *representational effect* ("*effet de représentation*") exerted at the level of the representations through the influence of the situation and environment upon the state of the conditions of production out of which those representations are elaborated. Finally, the third type is a *discursive effect* ("*effet de discours*") exerted at the level of the assertion process through the differences between representations and generators connected to them.

Many aspects of this model are still entirely hypothetical, even though they appear to gain support from convergent developments in linguistic theory and in the theories of ideological and social relations. The existence of discursive effects is certainly the weakest and most unexplored point in the model, and at the same time the part which is most directly related to the traditional field of social psychology. However, at present we are developing an experimental program in order to seek some empirical support for this part of the model.

REFERENCES

Bellert, I. (1968). "On a condition of the coherence of texts." WDN. Zam. 146/0/68 University of Warsaw, Poland. Mimeo.

Culioli, A. (1968). La formalisation en linguistique, *Cahiers pour l'Analyse* **9**, 106–117.

Frege, G. (1892, 1966). On sense and reference. Über Sinn und Bedeutung. *In* "Philosophical Writings of Gottlob Frege," pp. 56–78. Blackwell, Oxford. (First published in *Z. Phil. Philosoph. Kritik* **100**, 25–50.)

Herzlich, C. (1969). "Institutions hospitalières, pratiques médicales et insertion du malade à l'hôpital." Laboratoire de Psychologie Sociale de l'E.P.H.E., Paris. Mimeo.

Jakobson, R. (1957). "Shifters, verbal categories and the Russian verb." Russian Language Project, Department of Slavic Languages and Literature, Harvard University.

Jakobson, R. (1960). Closing statements: Linguistics and poetics. *In* "Style in Language" (T. A. Sebeok, ed.), pp. 350–377. MIT Press, Cambridge, Mass., U.S.A.

Moscovici, S. (1961). "La Psychanalyse, son Image et son Public: Étude sur la Représentation Sociale de la Psychanalyse," Presses Universitaires de France, Paris.

Moscovici, S. (1967). Communication processes and the properties of language. *In* "Advances in Experimental Social Psychology" (Berkowitz, ed.), Vol. III, pp. 225–270, Academic Press, New York and London.

Pêcheux, M. (1969). "Vers l'Analyse Automatique du Discours. Dunod," Paris.

Plon, M. (1969). Quelques aspects des processus d'identification dans une situation expérimentale, *Bull. du C.E.R.P.* **18**, 2, 99–116.

Reichenbach, H. (1947). "Elements of Symbolic Logic," Collier-Macmillan, Toronto.

Rommetveit, R. (1968). "Words, Meanings and Messages," Academic Press, New York.

Wiener, M. and Mehrabian, A. (1968). "Language within Language: Immediacy, a Channel of Communication," Appleton, New York.

Causal Attribution in Messages as a Function of Inter-message Semantic Relations

GUIDO PEETERS

The constituents of verbal messages, as defined by Rommetveit (1966), are the message *sender*, the *receiver*, and the *designatum*. Study of the transmission of messages falls at the intersection of psycholinguistics and social psychology. The present study is an attempt to apply social psychological *attribution theory* (Heider, 1958; Kelley, 1967) to the understanding of how verbal messages are integrated into the life space of a *receiver*. The substance of *attribution theory* is that a perceiver tends to increase consistency in his life space by assuming that there are causal relations between covarying phenomena. When applied to information processing, the theory implies that the message receiver tends to attribute the cause of any variations between messages to variations between relevant constituents of his life space. For example, when a *receiver* is confronted with two different messages like *X is white* and *X is black*, he can integrate them in a consistent way by making one of the following three assumptions:

1. The messages reflect the opinions either of two different persons, or of the same person in different circumstances (*attribution to sender*).
2. The messages reflect opinions concerning either different objects X and Y or different aspects of one object Z (*attribution to designatum*).
3. At least one of the messages was misunderstood (*attribution to receiver*).

This study deals only with attribution to *sender* and *designatum*. It *focuses* on responses of the message *receiver* which result from his reaction to the formal semantic relations existing between messages presented to him. Specifically, the problem dealt with is whether, as a result of the formal semantic relations existing between two messages, the receiver tends to attribute the two different messages, either to two different *senders* who are speaking about the same *designatum* (*sender-attribution*), or to a single *sender* who is speaking about two different *designata* (*designatum-attribution*). Three semantic relations are considered:

1. *Equivalence:* the messages imply each other; e.g. *X is white/X has the colour of snow.*
2. *Compatibility* (without *equivalence*): the truths of the messages are unrelated; e.g. *X is white/X is angular.*
3. *Incompatibility:* the messages cannot both be true; e.g. *X is black/ X is white.*

There is an increasing degree of variation in the messages from *equivalence* to *incompatibility*. On the other hand, more variation may be expected within the class of *designata* than within the class of *senders*, the former including the latter. By virtue of the tendency toward perceived covariation between cause and effect assumed by *attribution theory*, more attribution to the *designatum* may be expected in the *incompatibility* condition than in the *compatibility* condition, amd more in the latter than in the *equivalence* condition.

In order to test this hypothesis and to explore the field further, two experiments, a pilot study and a final experiment, were carried out. Semantic relations were operationalized using adjectives from the semantic differential (Osgood *et al.*, 1957). Adjectives with high loadings on the same factor, and with equivalent signs, were labelled *equivalent*; adjectives with high loadings on unrelated factors were labelled *compatible*; finally adjectives with high loadings on the same factor but with opposite signs were labelled *incompatible*. Although this operationalization probably does not realize perfectly the theoretical definition of the semantic relations involved, it seems to be a useful approximation because it enables one to test the theory in the subtle field of affective meaning. Moreover, in real life situations a perfect realization of semantic relations may seldom occur.

THE PILOT STUDY

Method

Two parallel sets of six different messages were constructed. Each message consisted of two synonymous adjectives which were highly loaded for Flemish subjects with Osgood's factors of affective meaning according to Jakobovits (1966): E(valuation), A(ctivity), and P(otency). As is shown in Table 1, for each factor within each set, there were two messages with opposite loadings ($+$ and $-$), the positive adjectives being the scale opposites of the negative ones in the semantic differential. The messages were combined into six pairs with *equivalent* messages, twelve

TABLE 1

Sets of messages

Set 1	Set 2
1. $E+$ aggreable, cosy	$E'+$ pleasant, magnificent
2. $E-$ disagreeable, cheerless	$E'-$ boring, horrible
3. $A+$ bloody, active	$A'+$ quick, sharp
4. $A-$ not bloody, passive	$A'-$ slow, blunt
5. $P+$ long, deep	$P'+$ big, strong
6. $P-$ short, shallow	$P'-$ small, weak

with *compatible* messages, and six with *incompatible* messages (see Table 2 "Pairs"). Although it was possible to construct these message-pairs using the messages from only one set, messages from two sets were used in order to avoid identical lexical expressions (agreeable/agreeable) and scale opposites (agreeable/disagreeable) within a single message-pair.

Each message-pair was presented on a card. The subjects were told that the messages on the cards represented "impressions" uttered by persons and that they referred to "objects" which could be things, persons, situations, etc. The two impressions on a card could either stem from *two* different persons and be related to a *single* object (*sender-attribution*), or they could stem from a *single* person but be related to *two* different objects (*designatum-attribution*). Both alternatives are illustrated by simple diagrams in Fig. 1 in which the persons are represented by

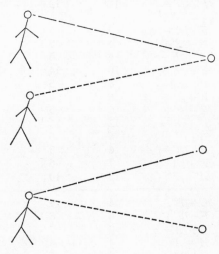

FIG. 1. The diagrams represent *sender-attribution* (upper diagram) and *designatum-attribution* (lower diagram).

very schematic human figures, the objects by circles, and the impressions by dotted lines connecting person and object. In individual sessions, 18 Flemish subjects (psychological staff members and completely naïve subjects) were asked to match cards with diagrams according to their first impressions. They were informed that the number of cards for each alternative was unlimited, and that all cards might even belong to one and the same alternative.

Results and Discussion

In Table 2 the total number of *sender-attributions* is presented for each message-pair. The corresponding number of *designatum-attributions* can be obtained by subtracting the number of a given column from the

TABLE 2

Number of sender-attributions for pairs of messages with different semantic relations

Semantic relations	Pairs	Pilot study N = 18	Experiment N = 20	Reliability data N = 15	
				1st Session	2nd Session
Equival.	$E+/E'+$	14	19	14	13
	$E'-/E-$	15	19	14	14
	$A+/A'+$	12	14	11	12
	$A'-/A-$	12	13	11	13
	$P+/P'+$	11	9	8	9
	$P'-/P-$	12	13	11	8
Compat.	$E+/A+$	5	5	4	7
	$A-/E'+$	4	7	5	4
	$A'+/E-$	6	6	4	5
	$E'-/A'-$	10	14	12	13
	$P+/E+$	8	5	4	4
	$E'+/P-$	6	4	3	5
	$E-/P'+$	8	5	4	8
	$P'-/E'-$	12	11	9	11
	$A+/P+$	6	6	5	7
	$P-/A'+$	6	5	4	5
	$P'+/A-$	7	6	4	5
	$A'-/P'-$	13	10	9	9
Incompat.	$E+/E'-$	4	9	7	5
	$E-/E'+$	6	8	4	6
	$A+/A'-$	3	3	2	3
	$A-/A'+$	4	4	3	3
	$P+/P'-$	3	5	3	4
	$P-/P'+$	1	2	1	3

total number of subjects whose attributions are considered (shown at the head of each column). Thus a low number of *sender-attributions* corresponds to a high number of *designatum-attributions*, and vice versa. Results from the pilot study also are shown in Table 2. They are consistent with *attribution theory*. In the *equivalence* condition the number of subjects who attribute to the *sender* ranges from 11 to 15 (M = 12·7), in the *compatibility* condition it ranges from 4 to 13 (M = 7·6), and in the *incompatibility* condition from 1 to 6 (M = 3·5). When the subjects are considered individually, it results that for 11 of the 18 subjects the number of *sender-attributions* is ranked in the expected way over the three conditions. This is highly significant because the random value would only be 18/3! = 3 instead of 11.

When message-pairs within conditions are considered, it results that pairs consisting of two evaluative messages tend to elicit more *sender-attributions* than the remaining pairs within the same condition. In the *equivalence* condition, the two evaluative pairs yield 14 and 15 *sender-attributions* respectively, while the four remaining pairs yield a maximum of 12 *sender-attributions*. An analogous trend can be observed in the *incompatibility* condition. In a more detailed analysis, evaluative pairs were compared with activity- and potency-pairs in both *equivalence* and *incompatibility* conditions. The resulting four comparisons are:

1. Evaluative with activity-pairs in *equivalence* condition (EA–Eq).
2. Evaluative with potency-pairs in *equivalence* condition (EP–Eq).
3. Evaluative with activity-pairs in *incompatibility* condition (EA–Inc.).
4. Evaluative with potency-pairs in *incompatibility* condition (EP–Inc.).

In order to apply sign tests subjects were taken as units; +1 was assigned to each subject with more *sender-attributions* for the two evaluative message-pairs than for the two non-evaluative message-pairs, while −1 was assigned to each subject with fewer *sender-attributions* for the two evaluative message-pairs than for the two non-evaluative ones. When there was no predominance of one kind of message-pair over the other, no sign was attributed. Thus when a subject yielded a *sender-attribution* for each of the two evaluative message-pairs in the *equivalence* condition, while he yielded only one *sender-attribution* and one *designatum-attribution* for the two activity-pairs within the same condition, a plus sign (+1) was noted for the EA–Eq comparison. In all four comparisons, positive signs were more predominant than negative signs: EA–Eq yielded +8 against −3; EP–Eq, +6 against −2; EA–Inc., +5 against −3; and EP–Inc., +4 against −0. This confirms that evaluative message-pairs tend to elicit more *sender-attributions* than other message-pairs. In none of the four comparisons, however, is the predominance significant.

Finally, it should be noted that the number of *sender-attributions* for individual subjects ranged from 4 to 15. It might be that some subjects are more inclined to *sender-attribution*, while others are more inclined to *designatum-attribution*. The data available, however, are quite inconclusive as the sample is small and information concerning reliability is lacking.

FINAL EXPERIMENT

The pilot study yielded overwhelming evidence for the impact of inter-message semantic relations upon the cognitive integration of the messages in the life space. This impact is strongly consistent with *attribution theory*. Moreover, it was suggested that the attribution process might be influenced by the quality of the meaning of the messages (evaluative or non-evaluative), and by inter-individual differences. In order to obtain more evidence, a final experiment was performed. It is an exact replication of the pilot study, with the exception that the subjects were 20 male Flemish students from the various faculties of the University of Louvain, K.U.L., Belgium. Another change was that in order to test reliability, the procedure was unexpectedly repeated one week after the first session. Hypotheses were derived from the main outcomes of the pilot study.

Hypothesis 1

Consistent with *attribution theory*, *sender-attributions* would increase from *incompatibility*, through *compatibility*, to the *equivalence* condition.

Hypothesis 2

In both *incompatibility* and *equivalence* conditions evaluative message-pairs would elicit more *sender-attributions* than non-evaluative ones.

Hypothesis 3

There would be reliable inter-individual differences concerning number of *sender-attributions*.

Results:

The number of *sender-attributions* for all 20 subjects are presented in Table 2 under "Experiment". Only 15 of the 20 subjects could be reached again for the second session. Their results from both first and second sessions are presented under "Reliability Data". The subgroup of 15 subjects seems to be quite representative for the whole group, the rank correlation between the columns "Experiment" and "Reliability Data 1st Session" being 0·97.

Hypothesis 1

Again the results are strongly consistent with *attribution theory*. The number of *sender-attributions* increases from the *incompatibility* condition (range: from 2 to 9; Mean $= 5\cdot2$) through *compatibility* condition (range: from 4 to 14; Mean $= 7$) to *equivalence* condition (range: from 9 to 19; Mean $= 14\cdot5$). The data are quite reliable, the rank correlation between the data in columns representing the 1st Session and 2nd Session being $0\cdot89$. Furthermore, when subjects are considered individually, the hypothesis is confirmed once more. Thirteen of the 20 subjects yielded numbers of *sender*-attributions which were ranked over the three conditions in the way the hypothesis predicted, while the randomly expected number would be only $20/3! = 3\cdot33$. This finding is also reliable. Seven of the 15 subjects who were retested yielded ranks consistent with the hypothesis in *both* sessions, while only one subject switched from a consistent rank in the first session to an inconsistent one in the second session.

Hypothesis 2

The data from the final experiment, like those from the pilot study, are consistent with Hypothesis 2 (see Table 2); within conditions, evaluative message-pairs tend to elicit more *sender-attributions* than non-evaluative ones. However, when the sign test analysis (explained in the "Pilot Study") is applied, the hypothesis is confirmed: EA–Eq yields $+9$ against 0 ($p = 0\cdot002$), EP–Eq yields $+11$ against -1 ($p = 0\cdot003$), EA–Inc yields $+8$ against -1 ($p = 0\cdot02$), and EP–Inc. yields $+9$ against -2 ($p = 0\cdot033$). The same analysis applied to the reliability data leads to analogous, but less significant results (p ranges from $0\cdot03$ to $0\cdot35$). These results, however, could be due to the decrease of degrees of freedom. It should be noted that the one-tailed tests used in this experiment are justified by the nature of the hypothesis.

Hypothesis 3

For each of the 20 subjects, the individual number of *sender-attributions* ranged from 4 to 16; for the 15 who were retested they ranged from 8 to 16 in the first session, and from 8 to 15 in the second session. The rank correlation between both sessions is quite low: $0\cdot40$. A closer examination of the data shows that the *compatibility* data are particularly unreliable ($0\cdot13$), while more favourable rank correlations were found for *incompatibility* ($0\cdot76$) and *equivalence* data ($0\cdot52$). Although the latter coefficients, however, remain too low to prove reliability, they draw attention to a new differential effect of the conditions which should be the object of further research. Consistent with Hypothesis 3 is the finding that all 11 subjects whose responses were consistent with Hypothesis 1 in the second session had responded in the same manner in the first session; there was only one subject who only responded consistently with Hypothesis 1 in one session. All together, the data concerning the third hypothesis remain rather inconclusive, which suggests that further research is required.

CONCLUSION

The main contribution of the present study is that it attempts to bring the fields of social psychology and psycholinguistics closer together. A linguistic variable like semantic relation has been shown to influence information processing in a way which is consistent with *attribution theory*, a contribution of social psychology. At the same time, the study tends to validate Osgood's affective meaning system and the semantic relations operationalized by means of this system. Moreover, it yields material which may lead to a better understanding of Osgood's concepts. Here not only the promotion of *sender-attributions* by evaluative messages should be mentioned, but also some of the enigmatic outcomes shown in Table 2, like the high scores for pairs $E'-/A'-$, $P'-/E'-$, and $A'-/P'-$, may be relevant.

Finally, it should be noted that the study may have many applications in classic social psychology where it may lead to new insights into research. For instance, conforming behaviour may often be conceived of as a means of escaping from a cognitive conflict which is aroused by a barred tendency toward *designatum-attribution*. Indeed, in many experiments on conformity, the subject is confronted with an *incompatibility* relation between the message he would emit spontaneously and the messages he receives from his peers which, according to the experiments reported above, would induce a tendency toward *designatum-attribution*. At the same time, however, the experimental setting induces the conflicting information that the peers are dealing with the same designatum as subjects, which excludes *designatum-attribution*. When subject conforms, the *incompatibility* relation inducing the conflicting tendency toward *designatum-attribution* is dissipated. If this analysis is correct, conformity behaviour may be expected to be a function of the factors which according to the present study would influence *sender-* and *designatum-attribution*.

REFERENCES

Heider, F. (1958). "The Psychology of Interpersonal Relations," John Wiley and Sons, New York.

Jakobovits, L. A. (1966). Comparative psycholinguistics in the study of cultures, *Internat. J. Psychol.* **1,** 15–37.

Kelley, H. H. (1967). Attribution theory in social psychology. Report prepared for the Nebraska Symposium on Motivation.

Osgood, C. E., Suci, G. J. and Tannenbaum, P. H. (1957). "The measurement of meaning." University of Illinois Press, Urbana.

Rommetveit, R. (1966). Linguistic and non-linguistic components of communication: Notes on the intersection of psycholinguistics and social psychological theory. Paper delivered at the Third European Conference on Experimental Social Psychology at Royamont.

Part III

INTRALINGUISTIC CONTEXT: WORD ORDER,
IMPRESSION FORMATION, AND RETENTION

INTRODUCTION TO PAPERS BY JASPARS *ET AL.* AND WOLD

Chronologically speaking, the first study of impression formation with an explicit psycholinguistic perspective and a focus upon intralinguistic context was Wold's study, of which only a partial progress report is included in the present monograph (pp. 127–138). The data reported by Wold are a small part of a set of experimental data to be reported separately in a more comprehensive study of word order, strategies of decoding, and retention. The somewhat cryptic form of Wold's report and emphasis on particular problems of interpretation are due to the fact that it was presented at the Oslo seminar on psycholinguistics in response to a fairly detailed presentation of the experiment conducted at the Louvain training seminar which follows. The Wold experiments, however, had been conducted before the study by Jaspars *et al.* (pp. 109–125) which appears first in this section of the monograph.

One of the major points of comparison between the two studies is the effects of pre- versus post-position of adjectives on the retrieval of these adjectives. Wold did not construct the stimulus material with the primary purpose of assessing the impact of word order on impression formation quantitatively in terms of semantic differential scales. Such an assessment was attempted in the experiment by Jaspars *et al.* which in other respects is a modified replication of the as yet unpublished work by Wold. Skjerve's work (pp. 139–142) is chronologically the latest contribution to this interrelated set of experiments on intralinguistic contextual arrangement, decoding and recall, and the experiment was conducted as part of his graduate course work in psycholinguistics at the University of Oslo.

Order Effects in Impression Formation:
A Psycholinguistic Approach

JOS JASPARS, RAGNAR ROMMETVEIT, MALCOLM COOK,
NENAD HAVELKA, PAUL HENRY, WERNER HERKNER,
MICHEL PÊCHEUX, GUIDO PEETERS[a]

Impression formation research began with Asch's work in 1946. Since that time a large number of studies have been devoted to the problem of order effects in this work. In Experiment VI of his original study, Asch (1946) presented the same trait list twice, but the second time in reversed order. It was found that the first traits in the stimulus list had

[a] This work resulted from combined efforts of the authors at the European Research Training Seminar in Experimental Social Psychology. University of Louvain, 1967.

a greater impact upon the final impression than the traits at the end of the list. According to Asch, for most subjects the first terms set up a valence, which then exerts a continuous effect on the later terms.

Luchins (1958) also obtained a clear primacy effect for a two part personality description of a fictitious individual; however, he was able to show that the primacy effect decreased when a warning against it was given before or in between two opposing parts of the description. A recency effect, on the other hand, was obtained when an interpolated task had to be performed. By increasing the time interval between the two parts of the description from five to seventeen minutes, the recency effect was magnified. Luchins (1958) also found a recency effect when a questionnaire was administered after each of the two opposing parts of the description.

Anderson (1965), however, found consistent recency effects, as predicted by a linear opinion change model developed by Anderson and Hovland (1957). In Anderson's (1965) experiment, subjects were required to judge the innocence or guilt of an indicated person after the presentation of each argument. In subsequent experiments (Anderson and Barrios, 1961; Anderson and Hubert, 1963; Stewart, 1965; Jaspars, 1966), it was shown that response mode affects the total impression. If only one final impression is required, a primacy effect is usually obtained; if, however, the subjects are required to report cumulative impressions after each additional adjective, a recency effect is obtained. The explanation of the difference in results between these two conditions arises from the assumption that information which appears later in a series is less effective for one of a number of reasons; it may be because less attention is paid to it (Anderson and Hubert, 1963) or because such information is less novel (Schultz, 1963) or even that later information interferes with previous information (Hovland, 1957; Luchins, 1958). According to the theory, when the subject is asked to give an impression after each additional adjective, attention is shifted towards the end of the series and a recency effect is obtained. The same effect may be obtained by asking the subject to *recall* the adjectives used in the description of a person, in addition to forming a personality impression response.

In a more recent experiment, Anderson (1965) elaborated the theory and developed a generalized order paradigm to describe the results of impression formation experiments by giving differential weights to the adjectives according to their position in a series. Studies on conflict resolution in impression formation (Asch, 1946; Kastenbaum, 1951; Haire and Grunes, 1950; Pepitone and Hayden, 1955; Gollin, 1954) suggest, however, that the decrease in attention is not only a function of serial position, but also a function of the degree to which new information is in conflict with an already formed impression. Still other explanations have been offered for order effects in the impression formation work (Miller and Campbell, 1959; Lana, 1964). However, there is yet another important factor which needs to be taken into account. In all the studies discussed above the formation of impressions of completely abstract persons (Mr. or Mrs. A or X) has been studied; the person to whom the traits belong is never explicitly mentioned.

Rommetveit (1968, p. 250) has also given us some possible explanations for the order effects found. He suggests that a primacy effect could be explained by a tacit presupposition of isomorphy between *temporal order* and *order of importance*. In a spoken sequence of trait names describing another person, the last trait mentioned borders on a set of adjectives which essentially are not mentioned at all. Thus it may be that order effects in impression formation reveal pragmatic rules of language. Where grammar leaves the speaker with options, he may spontaneously choose word orders which maximize specific effects on the part of the listener. Such effects, moreover, must depend upon the way in which the listener decodes the entire message (Rommetveit and Turner, 1967). If, for example, he already has a certain knowledge of the *type of entity* which will be described before its attributes are made known, he will be able to decode the message in a cumulative fashion. Each additional adjective may in a way be tagged onto, and modify, an already amalgamated semantic entity. This, it should be recalled, is the situation with which subjects in impression formation studies are usually confronted. The entity (some *person*) is presupposed by the subject simply because it is mentioned in an abstract way by the experimenter in the instructions. An entirely different situation arises, however, when the entity to be modified is not known by the recipient of the message *at the beginning*. The final decoding in this case must be postponed until some noun has been heard, as the number of adjectives does not ordinarily exceed the span of short-term memory. Then at the moment of final decoding the first adjectives should be less available than those appearing just before the noun. Hence, in this situation we may expect a recency effect and retroactive modification of word meaning. Both processes have been symbolized in Fig. 1, taken from Rommetveit and Wold (1967).

In general we hypothesize, therefore, that a primacy effect will occur if a descriptive series of adjectives is preceded by a noun and that a recency effect will occur if the noun appears after the adjectives. Thus if we construct a series of adjectives, gradually increasing or decreasing in favourableness, we expect that in the noun-first situation the total impression in the ascending presentation (starting from the negative end) will tend to be more negative and the total impression in the descending presentation will tend to be more positive. If the noun appears at the end of the series, the total impression in the ascending order will be more favourable than the total impression in the descending order.

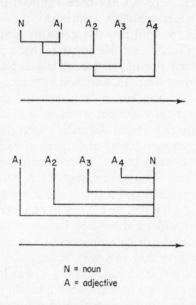

N = noun
A = adjective

FIG. 1. A schematic representation of decoding in the *noun-first* and *noun-end* conditions. Noun-first: cumulative decoding; noun-end: postponed decoding.

The two hypothesized strategies of decoding should also affect memory storage. Suppose, for instance, that the subject has listened to a series of descriptions. Then afterwards he is given one particular noun as a prompt word and asked to reproduce the adjectives that went with it. In this case, we would expect that a cumulative decoding (noun-first) will make for greater cohesion between noun and adjectives and hence for superior recall. In the *noun-end* condition the adjectives have to be stored separately in short-term memory until the noun is heard. Hence, a greater memory loss and more confusion with adjectives that are attached to *other nouns* in the series of descriptions are to be expected. Such expectations concerning overall recall have been confirmed in the experiments by Wold (1971, pp. 127–138).

If, moreover, correspondence is assumed between decoding strategy, impression formation, and recall (although such an assumption is very dubious in view of Anderson and Hubert's 1963 data), it is hypothesized that the adjective appearing closest to the noun will be recalled best. Accordingly, a primacy effect in recall is expected in the *noun-first* condition and recency effect in the *noun-end* condition.

It should be noted, however, that when a list of adjectives differing in favourableness is presented, it may be easier to recall the adjectives which have the most extreme scores in favourableness. At least in a study by Jaspars (1966, p. 52), it was found that subjects assign greater weight to extreme adjectives in an impression formation task regardless of the position of these adjectives in a trait list. This result could be explained by assuming that extreme adjectives are also recalled better. Since these adjectives would come either at the beginning or the end of the series, this effect may be magnified by the well-established interference effect in rote learning where the middle of a list is usually less well recalled than the beginning and the end. The order effect predicted here would be superimposed upon such accentuated serial position effects.

The hypotheses, more precisely formulated, are:

Hypothesis 1

The position of the noun in the description will affect impression formation. When the noun appears before the adjectives, the adjectives appearing first will contribute most to the total impression (primacy effect). When the noun comes at the end, the last adjectives will contribute most (recency effect).

Hypothesis 2

When the noun is presented before the series of adjectives, overall recall of the adjectives will be better than when the noun is presented after the series of adjectives.

Hypothesis 3

Adjectives will be recalled better the closer they are to the noun, i.e. a recency effect in recall will occur in the *noun-end* condition and a primacy effect in the *noun-first* condition.

Hypothesis 4

More confusions will occur between the adjectives belonging to different stimulus nouns in the *noun-end* condition than in the *noun-first* condition, i.e. the proportion of stimulus adjectives that are attached to the wrong noun in retrieval should be higher when the noun comes at the end.

METHOD

Subjects

The subjects were 120 Belgian soldiers from the Kwartier Cdt de Hemptinne in Heverlee. They were divided into 6 groups of 20 subjects each for the experimental conditions. The soldiers came to the Laboratory for Experimetal Social Psychology at the Psychological Institute of the University of Louvain where the experiment was carried out as part of a training seminar in experimental social psychology.

Stimulus Material

The stimulus materials consisted of descriptions made up of four adjectives and a noun. Five sets of four adjectives were constructed from a list of 20 adjectives. Evaluation scores for the 20 adjectives had been obtained from a comparable population in a previous study (Jaspars, 1966). The five adjective series were constructed in such a way that the average evaluation score was approximately neutral on a combined 7-point evaluation scale; thus the position of the adjectives in each series was determined by their evaluation score.

The nouns which were used in combination with the adjective sets were all occupational titles. The nouns were selected from a pretest in which 14 Belgian soldiers rated 20 occupational titles on five 7-point scales from Osgood's semantic differential (Osgood *et al.*, 1957). Ten occupations were selected on the following bases:

1. A small variance of the evaluation ratings of an occupation

2. Neutral scores on the non-evaluation scales (between -1 and $+1$)

3. The selected occupations differed as little as possible in evaluation

The resulting set of ten occupations were used in a second pretest which was designed to produce a credible combination of trait list and occupation for each description. A group of 15 Belgian soldiers was asked to indicate for each of the occupations what combination of trait names was most likely to be expected in a person of that occupation. The subjects were given a set of five envelopes, to which booklets with the four adjectives of a trait list were attached and a set of 10 slips of paper on which the occupational titles were printed. The order of the adjectives in the booklets was varied systematically; the order of the pages in the booklet represented an ascending order of evaluation for one half of the subjects and a descending order for the others. By putting the slips of paper into the envelopes, subjects were to indicate for each occupational title which series would most be expected in a person of that occupation.

The final set of adjectives and nouns used in the experiment were:

1. a dishonest, gloomy, self-confident, helpful *sailor*;
2. an uncongenial, suspicious, punctual, reliable *doctor*;
3. a lethargic, jealous, cheerful, cordial *mannequin*;
4. an opinionated, shy, impulsive, friendly *shop assistant*;
5. a rude, thick-skinned, broad-minded, sociable *carpenter*.

In order to counteract a sustained set for "person description", that is a belief that all adjectives applied to a human being, two "thing" descriptions were used. One of them was presented as one of two introductory examples and the other appeared between the second and third experimental items. It was thus intended that subjects would have no definite knowledge of the entity being described before it was heard.

Design

The design of the experiment is shown in Table 1. The position of the noun in the adjective-noun description was either the first position or the last; in a third, control condition the noun was omitted leaving just an

TABLE 1

Design of experiment

		Order of adjectives	
		Ascending	Descending
Position of noun	Noun first	N = 20	N = 20
(Occupation)	Noun end	N = 20	N = 20
Control	No noun	N = 20	N = 20

adjective list. The other major variable was the ordering of adjectives with respect to their valence or scores on the evaluative scale of the Semantic Differential. In one case the order was one of ascending or increasing valence and in the other of descending valence.

Procedure

The experiment was presented to all 20 subjects in each condition simultaneously, and was completed in one day. The subjects were seated well apart in a lecture room. The experimenter briefly explained the nature of the experiment and proceeded with the instructions after the subjects had been given booklets. The instructions dealt with the use of rating scales in the impression formation part of the experiment. The subjects were *not* told that they would be asked to recall the adjectives. On each page of the first part of the booklet five rating scales were presented, three of which were evaluation scales to be used in the analysis and two of which functioned as buffer scales. The stimulus material itself was presented by a tape recorder. The tape-recorded series of adjective-noun combinations were pronounced by a person who had a voice which was distinctly different from the voice of the experimenter.

The five stimulus series were presented in the same order in each condition. After the presentation of each stimulus, the subjects were given 30 seconds to rate their impression on the five scales on each page in the booklet. After the impression formation part of the experiment, the subjects in the experimental conditions were asked to recall the adjectives of each of the occupations mentioned during the first part of the experiment. On each of the subsequent pages of the booklets the occupational title was printed in the appropriate place for that condition and a blank was left to fill in whatever the subject thought he remembered about a certain description. The whole procedure lasted for about 20 minutes.

RESULTS

Primacy and Recency Effects in Impression Formation

The first hypothesis suggested that the position of the noun in the description would affect the total impression which was based upon the combination of noun and adjectives. It was hypothesized that a primacy effect would be found when the noun appears before the adjectives and a recency effect would be found when the noun comes at the end. The results of the impression formation part of the experiment which are relevant to this hypothesis are presented in Table 2 and Fig. 2.

TABLE 2

Total impressions
Combined evaluative ratings on three scales

Noun position	Order of adjectives	Sailor	Doctor	Stimulus Shop assistant	Car- penter	Manne- quin	Total
No noun	Ascending	+0·68	−0·05	+0·49	+0·31	+0·19	+0·32
	Descending	−0·91	+0·53	+0·00	−0·28	−0·15	−0·16
Noun-first	Ascending	−0·22	+0·78	+0·50	+0·63	−0·15	+0·31
	Descending	−0·35	+0·42	−0·10	−0·17	−0·63	−0·17
Noun-end	Ascending	+0·30	+1·28	+1·03	+1·00	−0·07	+0·71
	Descending	−0·57	+0·03	+0·35	+0·13	−0·47	−0·11

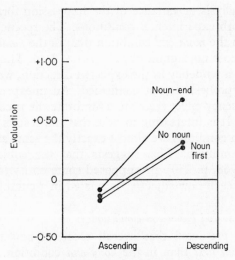

FIG. 2. Total impressions.

The row totals of Table 2 show that, contrary to the hypothesis, a recency effect occurs for all stimuli in both *noun-first* and *noun-end* conditions as the total impressions based upon the ascending combinations are more positive in all cases than the total impressions for the descending combinations. This effect $[F\ (1,76) = 16\cdot31,\ df = 1]$ is significant at the $p < 0\cdot01$ level, as can be seen in Table 3 where the

TABLE 3

Analysis of variance of impression formation data

	d.f.	M.S.	F	
Between subjects	79			
Noun-first—Noun-end	1	48·0	2·09	
Ascending/Descending	1	374·0	16·31	$p < 0\cdot01$
Noun-first, Noun-end × Ascending/Descending	1	26·0	1·14	
Error between subjects	76	22·93		
Within subjects				
Stimuli	4	131·5	6·61	$p < 0\cdot01$
Stimuli × *Noun-first, Noun-end*	4	5·75		
Stimuli × Ascending/Descending	4	5·50		
Stimuli × *Noun-first, Noun-end* × Ascending/Descending	4	8·75		
Stimuli within subject error	4	19·88		

results of the analysis of variance of the impression formation data are presented for both experimental conditions. The recency effect appears to be stronger in the *noun-end* condition than in the *noun-first* condition, but this difference is not significant, $F(1·76) = 1·14$. Therefore, although the results show a tendency in the expected direction, we must conclude that the first hypothesis is not confirmed. An unexpected overall and rather strong recency effect seems to adumbrate the predicted difference in order effects. It is interesting to note that the results obtained in the control, no-noun condition are almost exactly the same as those found in the *noun-first* condition. This suggests that the subject has, indeed (Rommetveit, 1968, p. 250), presupposed some entity (a person) in advance, to which each new adjective is related in a cumulative fashion.

Recall in Noun-first and Noun-end Condition

Hypothesis 2 predicted that overall recall of adjectives should be better in the *noun-first* than in the *noun-end* condition. Table 4 which gives the total number of correctly recalled adjectives in the different conditions shows that recall is better in the *noun-first* condition. Table 5 presents a summary of the analysis of variance and shows that this difference is significant, $F(1,76) = 15·21$, $p < 0·01$. Thus the second

TABLE 4

Number of correctly recalled adjectives

Position	Noun-first		Noun-end		Σ
	Ascending	Descending	Ascending	Descending	
1	18	17	6	5	46
2	19	9	12	1	41
3	4	20	1	15	40
4	27	25	12	15	79
Σ	68	71	31	36	206

hypothesis is clearly confirmed. When the noun precedes the adjectives, recall is much better than when the noun comes at the end. In the first condition the number of correctly recalled adjectives is about twice the number of correctly recalled adjectives in the second condition.

Distance from Noun

The analysis of variance presented in Table 5 shows that the third hypothesis is confirmed to a certain extent, also. According to the theory, a primacy effect in recall is to be expected in the *noun-first* condition, whereas a recency effect should occur in the *noun-end* condition. This

TABLE 5

Analysis of variance recall data

Source of variation	d.f.	M.S.	F	
Between subjects	79			
Noun-first—noun-end (position noun)	1	3.24	15·21	$p < 0.01$
Ascending/descending	1	0·04		
Position noun × Ascending/ descending	1	0·00		
Between subject error	76	0·213		
Within subjects				
Nature of stimulus	4	0·30	3·80	$p < 0.01$
Stimulus × Position noun	4	0·20	2·53	$p < 0.05$
Stimulus × Ascending/ descending	4	0·16	2·02	
Stimulus × Position noun × Ascending/descending	4	0·06		
Error within subject for stimulus	304	0·079		
Position of adjective	3	0·86	1·34	
Noun × Position adjective	3	0·16	8·00	$p < 0.01$
Ascending/descending × Position adjective	3	1·11	1·50	
Position noun × Ascending/ descending × Position adjective	3	0·02	2·00	
Error within subject for position adjective	228	0·102		
Position adjective × Nature of stimulus	12	0·64	7·03	$p < 0.01$
Position noun × Position adjective × Nature of stimulus	12	0·02		
Ascending/descending × Position adjective × Nature of stimulus	12	0·74	8·13	$p < 0.01$
Position noun × Ascending/ descending × Position adjective × Nature of stimulus	12	0·01		
Error within subject for position adjective × Nature of stimulus	912	0·091		

hypothesis implied that there should be an interaction effect in recall between position of adjectives (regardless of the nature of stimulus or the ascending or descending order) and the position of the noun with respect to the set of adjectives (*noun-first* versus *noun-end*). Tested against the appropriate second order interaction term it appears that this effect is significant, $F(3,12) = 8\cdot00$, $p < 0\cdot01$. Fig. 3 which presents the positional recall of adjectives in *noun-first* and *noun-end* conditions shows, however, that the interaction effect is much more complicated than expected. In the *noun-end* condition a clear recency effect occurs, but in

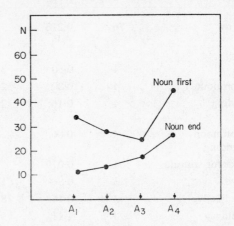

FIG. 3. Recall of adjectives in *noun-first* and *noun-end* conditions.

the *noun-first* condition a combined primacy and recency effect seems to occur, the recency effect being considerably stronger than the primacy effect. This result is in accordance with the results of the impression formation part of the study where a strong recency effect was found also.

The analysis of variance presented in Table 5 shows, moreover, that the results discussed above depend to some extent upon the nature of the stimulus material used. The effect of the position of the noun upon overall recall is much stronger for *the shop assistant, the carpenter* and *the mannequin* items than for the other two occupational titles. There is also an interaction effect between nature of stimulus and position of adjectives which is caused by the difference in positional recall in the description of *the mannequin* in comparison with all other noun-adjective combinations. The second order interaction effect which is related to this difference in positional recall shows that this difference is mainly due to the fact that the adjective "jealous" is recalled exceptionally well.

Confusions in Recall

The fourth hypothesis predicts that fewer intrusions from other adjectives will occur in the recall of the adjectives of a given noun in the *noun-first* than in the *noun-end* condition. To test this hypothesis an analysis of variance was made of the ratios of correctly recalled adjectives to the total number of adjectives recalled. The results are presented in Table 6 and Table 7.

TABLE 6

Mean ratio of correct to total recall of adjectives

	Noun-first	Noun-end	
Ascending order	0·786	0·622	0·707
Descending order	0·767	0·668	0·723
	0·776	0·644	

TABLE 7

Analysis of variance intrusions

Source	d.f.	M.S.	F
Noun-first—Noun-end	1	2·81	1·87
Ascending/Descending order	1	0·32	
Position noun × Order adjective	1	1·01	
Error	76	1·50	

Although the results shown in Table 6 and Table 7 are in the expected direction, it is quite clear that the difference in confusions between *noun-first* and *noun-end* conditions fails to reach an acceptable level of statistical significance $F(1·76) = 1·87$, *ns*.

DISCUSSION

The principal hypothesis of the present experiment stated that order effects in impression formation and recall are determined to a significant extent by the position of the noun with respect to the adjectives in the stimulus material. We hypothesized, moreover, that fewer confusions in recall would occur between different stimuli when the noun appeared in first position as opposed to last position, and that overall recall would be better in the *noun-first* than in the *noun-end* condition. Only the last hypothesis was clearly confirmed. The principal hypothesis requires, therefore, some further discussion.

As we have seen, a strong recency effect occurs both in impression formation and recall. This might possibly be interpreted as evidence for a *functional relationship* between memory and impression formation. Whereas Anderson and Hubert (1963) found a discrepancy between retrieval of adjectives and the contribution of those adjectives to the total impression, the present study suggests that the last appearing adjectives, being better retained in short-term memory during impression formation *and* more easily retrieved afterwards, contribute more than the other adjectives to the evaluative response. Since the evaluative scores of all adjectives in isolation are known from a previous study (Jaspars, 1966), the contribution of each of them to the total impression can be estimated by weighing its evaluative score on the basis of the recall data. In order to combine the results of different stimuli, we have to convert the predicted scores of the total impression of each stimulus in the four different conditions into standard scores. When this is done, a correlation between obtained and predicted total impressions of $r = + 0.44$ is obtained. Adjectives that were extreme with respect to emotive word meaning *and* also discrepant with the initial adjective describing the same entity always appeared in the last position in the present study. Hence, it might be argued that they were probably salient in short-term memory during impression formation and accordingly more easily retrieved during the subsequent recall task.

Such an explanation, however, is clearly contrary to the findings and explanations of Hovland (1957) and Luchins (1958) and it disregards some significant discrepancies between impression formation and recall data. There is, first of all, a significant *position of noun* $\times$ *position of adjectives* inter-action effect in recall (Table 5 and Fig. 3). This means, more specifically, that the overall recency effect has been partly over-ridden *in recall* by a primacy effect only when the noun appeared before the adjectives.

"Nature of stimulus" has a significant main effect on impression formation scores as well as on recall. In addition, however, it enters into three significant interaction effects (with *position of noun*; with *position of adjectives*; and with *position of adjectives* $\times$ *ascending/descending*) in the analysis of variance of *recall scores*, whereas none of the corresponding interaction effects are significant in the analysis of impression formation (Tables 3 and 5).

These findings can hardly be explained at all unless we attempt a systematic comparison between the impression formation and retrieval tasks. When forming an impression, the subject is dealing with one and only one adjective-noun combination at a time. In the retrieval situation, on the other hand, he is given a noun as a prompt word, and his task is to retrieve the adjectives that went with this particular noun from the entire set of adjective-noun combinations in memory storage. The very fact that *the noun* is used as a prompt then will accentuate the role of the variable "nature of stimulus"; confusion of stimulus items and memory loss is successfully avoided only to the extent the prompt word constitutes the nucleus of a very distinct entity. The *nature of stimulus* × *position of noun* interaction effect shows that distinctiveness of items revealed in differential retention of different items, is increased *when the noun appears first*. In this case it is possible to have acumulative strategy of decoding, with an immediate full decoding and "clarification" of every subsequent adjective and linkage of the attribute mediated by that adjective to the entity conveyed by the noun. Such a strategy is prohibited in the *noun-end* condition. The strong main effect of *position of noun* on recall thus must also be explained in terms of different strategies of decoding in the two main conditions. Re-encoding in the retrieval situation has to proceed from the noun, and success, to a large extent, is dependent upon the role of the noun during the initial decoding (cf. Fig. 1). This hypothesized effect of a cumulative versus a retroactive decoding strategy, however, should be considerably weaker (or even absent) in impression formation, since the whole adjective-noun combination is presumably available in immediate memory when the subject gives his evaluative response and the role of the noun as a clue to the adjectives that go with it, hence, is superfluous.

A final word may be said regarding the hypothesis which concerns the intrusions from elements of other stimuli in the recall data. We expected fewer intrusions in the *noun-first* than in the *noun-end* condition. As this hypothesis was not confirmed at an acceptable level of statistical significance, we might look for other evidence. If the adjectives are stored separately in short-term memory, one might expect that the adjectives are almost never recalled in combination over and above the associations one would predict on the basis of chance. Inspection of the data shows that in the *noun-end* condition, adjectives are remembered only 27% of the time in pairs, whereas in the *noun-first* condition this occurs in 47% of the cases. In both cases, however, the results do not significantly differ from chance. This means that in both conditions, the associations between adjectives are completely determined by the associations between the adjectives and the noun and no evidence has been found for a cumulative mechanism beyond such a noun-adjective linkage (cf. Fig. 1). The results of the study of Wold (1971, pp. 127–138) presented later show the importance of the noun as a nucleus in recall is even greater in the condition where an adjective is used as a prompt word instead of the noun. Other adjectives are almost never remembered unless the noun is remembered.

What remains as the major substantial finding is thus a definite impact of word order upon *recall*. The "deep structure" of noun-adjective combinations remains the same whether the noun appears first or at the end. The variation of word order in the present study thus does not introduce grammatical differences, such as that between *attribution* and *apposition* in the study by Rommetveit and Turner (1967). This study revealed *poor retention* of adjectives appearing after the noun (in apposition). The differences between the present experiment and the study by Rommetveit and Turner, however, are such that a comparison of results is very dubious; no unequivocal conclusions concerning the role of word order, as such, *versus* attribution/apposition can be drawn by comparing the recall data from the two studies. The *noun-first* condition in the present study is similar in certain important aspects to a non-linguistic context of *presupposition* (Rommetveit *et al.*, 1971, pp. 29–56). It might be that as decoding and recall of a whole utterance may be facilitated by a preceding non-linguistic event which sets the stage for its interpretation, so may the adjectives be immediately disambiguated (and recall facilitated) by a preceding noun. Such proactive clarification, whether caused by intra linguistic or extra linguistic elements, appears to facilitate decoding and retention of the verbally mediated message.

REFERENCES

Asch, S. E. (1946). Forming impressions of personality, *J. abnorm. soc. Psychol.* **41**, 258–290.

Anderson, N. H. (1965). Primacy effects in personality impression formation using a generalised order effect paradigm, *J. pers. soc. Psychol.* **2**, No. 1, 1–9.

Anderson, N. H. and Barrios, A. A. (1961). Primary effects in personality impression formation, *J. abnorm. soc. Psychol.* **63**, 346–350.

Anderson, N. H. and Hovland, C. I. (1957). The representation of order effects in communication research. *In* "The Order of Presentation in Persuasion" (C. I. Hovland, ed.), pp. 158–169. Yale University. Press, New Haven, Conn.

Anderson, N. H. and Hubert, S. (1963). Effects of concomitant verbal recall on order effects in personality impression formation, *J. verb. Learn. verb. Behav.* **2**, 379–391.

Gollin, E. S. (1954). Forming impressions of personality, *J. Pers.* **23**, 65–76.

Haire, M. and Grunes, W. F. (1950). Perceptual defenses: processes protecting an organised perception of another personality, *Hum. Relat.* **3**, 403–412.

Hovland, C. I. *et al.* (eds) (1957). "The Order of Presentation in Persuasion." Yale University Press, New Haven, Conn.

Jaspars, J. (1966). On social perception. Proefschrift ter verkrijging van de graad van Doctor in de Sociale Wetenschappen aan de Rijksuniversiteit te Leiden. Leiden.

Kastenbaum, Alice (1951). An experimental study of the formation of impressions of personality. Unpublished master's thesis, Graduate Faculty of Political and Social Science. New School for Social Research, New York.

Lana, R. E. (1964). Three theoretical interpretations of order effects in persuasive communications, *Psychol. Bull.* **61**, 314–320.

Luchins, Abraham S. (1958). Definitiveness of impression and primacy-recency in communication, *J. soc. Psychol.* **48**, 275–290.

Miller, N. and Campbell, D. T. (1959). Recency and primacy in persuasion as a function of the timing of speeches and measurements. *J. abnorm. soc. Psychol.* **59**, 1–9.

Osgood, C. E., Suci, T. and Tannenbaum, P. (1957). "The Measurement of Meaning," University of Illinois Press, Urbana Illinois.

Pepitone, A. and Hayden, R. G. (1955). Some evidence of conflict resolution in impression formation, *J. abnorm. soc. Psychol.* **51**, 302–307.

Rommetveit, R. (1968). "Words, Meanings and Messages," Academic Press, New York and London.

Rommetveit, R., Cook, M., Havelka, N., Henry, P., Herkner, W., Pêcheux, M. and Peeters, G. (1971). Processing of utterances in context. *In* "Social Contexts of Messages" (E. A. Carswell and R. Rommetveit, eds), pp. 29–56. Academic Press, London and New York.

Rommetveit, R. and Turner, Elizabeth A. (1967). A study of "chunking" in transmission of messages, *Lingua* **18**, 337–351.

Rommetveit, R. and Wold, Astri H. (1967). Studies of verbal message transmission. *In* "Studies of Symbolic Processes." A report from a research group at the University of Oslo. Unpublished Manuscript.

Schulz, D. P. (1963). Primacy—recency within a sensory variation framework, *Psychol. Rec.* **13**, 129–139.

Stewart, R. H. (1965). Effect of continuous responding on the order effect in personality impression formation, *J. pers. soc. Psychol.* **1**, No. 2, 161–165.

Wold, Astri H. (1971). Impression formation. A psycholinguistic approach. *In* "Social Contexts of Messages" (E. A. Carswell and R. Rommetveit, eds), pp. 127–138. Academic Press, London and New York.

Impression Formation:
A Psycholinguistic Approach

Progress Report

ASTRI HEEN WOLD

The present study is very similar to the Louvain impression formation study (Order Effects in Impression Formation: A Psycholinguistic Approach) just reported (see pp. 109–125). In an effort to avoid duplication, the present study will be described in a somewhat abbreviated form.

It will be recalled from the review of the literature on impression formation presented in the Louvain study that a large number of factors were shown to affect whether or not a primacy or recency effect is found in impression formation. The Louvain study and the present study have attempted to investigate yet another factor. This factor concerns the time or order relationship between the referent or noun described and the adjectives describing it. More specifically, in the present study, the position of the referent with respect to its descriptive adjectives is varied. In one case (noun-first), the referent noun is presented before the modifying adjectives and the listener knows at the onset what is being described; in the other case (noun-end), the presentation of the referent is postponed until the end of the description so that it is not readily apparent at the onset what the referent is. In an attempt to ensure uncertainty as to the entity being described in the noun-end condition, a wide variety of referent nouns have to be used.

In earlier studies, the subjects have known from the start what is being described. Thus the results of these studies are comparable only to the noun-first condition of the present work. It could also be mentioned that in almost every case a "person" has been the referent given either in the instruction or in the description proper (for an exception, see Anderson and Norman, 1964).

The focus on the noun-first/noun-end variable results from an interest in the importance of language processing interpretations of impression formation work. Rommetveit (1968) has suggested that the order effects found in the formation of impressions may be related to decoding strategies of the listener. If the listener has knowledge of or has been presented with the referent before its attributes are given, the speaker will be able to decode the attributes cumulatively. However, if the attributes precede the referent, it would seem likely that final decoding would be delayed until the referent is heard.

It is thus hypothesized that the position of the noun in the verbal description will affect the formation of an impression. More specifically, it is hypothesized that when a noun precedes a descriptive series of adjectives a primacy effect will occur, and when the noun follows the descriptive set of adjectives a recency effect will occur. In terms of recall of stimulus descriptions, it is hypothesized that recall will be better when the noun precedes the adjectives than in the reverse case. This is due to the fact that in the former condition the subject knows what the adjectives refer to prior to their presentation, i.e. they have a referent to which the adjectives can be tagged.[a]

METHOD

The present study in many ways resembles the experiment described in the Louvain Study, "Order Effects in Impression Formation" (see pp. 109–125). The study reported here, however, consists of two experiments (Experiment I and Experiment II) which differ with regard to the instructions given to the subjects and the method of stimulus recall.

EXPERIMENT I

Subjects

The subjects were Oslo University students. There were 20 subjects in each of four experimental conditions, totalling 80 subjects in all.

Stimulus Materials

The stimulus material consisted of 6 descriptions, each having five adjectives (*A*'s) and one noun (*N*). Three of the *N*'s belonged to the class of "*things*" and three belonged to the class of "*persons*". The five *A*'s which formed a set were considered to have different scores on an evaluative scale. However, there was no pretest of this, but rather only the

---

[a] The hypotheses given here, however, are not identical to the initial hypotheses. For more details of these see Rommetveit, R. and Wold, A. H., "Studies of verbal message transmission in Studies of Symbolic Processes. A report from a research group at the University of Oslo." Unpublished manuscript.

intuition of the author was used. The position of each A within the set was decided after a pretest in which subjects were asked to arrange the A's in "natural order". This method of construction made it rather a matter of chance what sort of "evaluative profile" the descriptions had. It turned out, however, that natural order was very close to a descending order.

Design

As in the Louvain study, there were four experimental conditions in a 2×2 design. The two experimental variables were *Noun Position (Noun-first* versus *Noun-end)* and *Order of adjectives* $(A_1 - A_5)$ and $(A_5 - A_1)$. The different orders of adjectives are not strictly ascending or descending orders as in the Louvain study, but are the same adjectives presented in contrasting orders.

Procedure

The procedure differed in some rather important respects from that of the Louvain study. The subjects were told in the initial instructions that at the end of the experiment they would be asked to recall as much as possible from the descriptions. Moreover, they were asked to rate their impression on a 7-point evaluative scale, having 4 seconds for each rating. The recall of each description was prompted by the presentation of the appropriate noun.

EXPERIMENT II

A total of 160 University of Oslo students participated in ExperimentII. There were 20 subjects in each of 8 experimental conditions. The design of this second experiment was essentially the same as that of Experiment I. However, this time the recall task was given after the subjects had finished the rating task, *without any prior warning*. In addition, two methods of recall were used with each of the four experimental conditions in Experiment I. Thus in Experiment II there were actually 8 experimental conditions in all. The two recall conditions differed in terms of what was used as a prompt word. In one condition, N was used as the prompt word (as was the case in Experiment I); in the other condition, the first A was used as the prompt word. This latter condition changed the task somewhat, in that it involved recalling the correct N in addition to the remainder of the A set rather than A's only.

RESULTS AND DISCUSSION

The number of correctly recalled A's (right A given back to right N prompt word) for the four different conditions of Experiment I is given in Table 1. As in the Louvain study, it was found that the recall of the A's was much better in the *Noun-first* condition than in the *Noun-end*

TABLE 1

Number of correctly recalled adjectives in Experiment I

| Position | Noun-first | | Noun-end | | |
	A_1–A_5	A_5–A_1	A_1–A_5	A_5–A_1	Σ
1	61	43	7	15	126
2	56	22	21	10	109
3	51	44	24	19	138
4	32	61	14	41	148
5	33	47	30	45	155
Σ	233	217	96	130	676

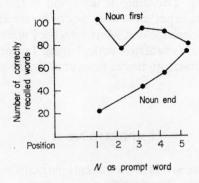

FIG. 1. Experiment I: Positional recall of adjectives in noun-first and noun-end conditions.

condition. Figure 1 shows the positional recall of A's. Notice that in contrast to the Louvain findings, a primacy effect or at least a tendency towards such an effect was found in the *Noun-first* conditions. In the *Noun-end* conditions, the results were essentially the same as those of the Louvain study. The fact that a primacy effect was found here, but not in the Louvain study, may be due to the different methods of stimulus construction and different instructions to the subjects. This would seem to be a likely explanation in view of the previously demonstrated sensitivity of impression formation order effects to experimental variables.

Table 2 gives the results of the ratings of the impressions or, more exactly, what these results show about primacy and recency effects. In one sense the results of the Louvain study and the present study are similar. In both studies the results of the recall task paralleled those of the impression formation task; but in the present study there was a stronger tendency toward primacy effects in the *Noun-first* conditions than in the Louvain study.

TABLE 2

Results from the impression formation task of Experiment I

Stimulus	Noun-first	Noun-end
Secretary	P	R
Chair	R	R
Movie	P	R
Actress	R	R
Farmer	P	—
Book	P	R

P = Primacy effect
R = Recency effect
— indicates no difference in average rating between A_1–A_5 and A_5–A_1

Table 3 shows the number of correctly recalled A's when N is given as prompt word in Experiment II. As before, the subjects in the *Noun-first* condition recalled the most A's, but as one might expect, they remembered less well than in Experiment I where they were warned of the reproduction task. Compare, however, the results from *Noun-end* in Table 1 and Table 3. Here the differences are surprisingly small. The total number of correctly reproduced A's in *Noun-end* conditions in Experiment I is 226 (96 + 130) and in Experiment II is 214 (99 + 115). This gives a difference of 12. The comparable difference for *Noun-first* conditions is 101. The analysis of variance reported in Table 4 gives $0.01 < p < 0.05$ for the interaction effect between position of N and instruction (In).

These results may shed some light on the process of decoding in the cases where N is given at the end of the description. The hypothesis suggests that the final decoding of the A's is dependent upon knowledge of N, which means that the A's must be stored in short-term memory until N is given. As a consequence, the subjects may be giving themselves some sort of self-instruction to try to remember the A's even when they are not expecting a recall task afterwards. In other words, implicit in the

TABLE 3

Number of correctly recalled adjectives. Noun used as prompt word. Experiment II

| Position | Noun-first | | Noun-end | | |
	A_1–A_5	A_5–A_1	A_1–A_5	A_5–A_1	Σ
1	38	33	15	14	100
2	41	13	31	9	94
3	36	35	19	30	120
4	23	57	4	30	114
5	27	46	30	32	135
Σ	165	184	99	115	563

TABLE 4

Analysis of variance of data from Experiments I and II

Source	Sum of squares	d.f.	Estimate	F	p
N	805·5063	1	805·5063	90·0963	$p < 0.001$
In	79·8063	1	79·8063	8·9264	$0.001 < p < 0.01$
A	17·5563	1	17·5563	1·964	
Within cells	1358·9500	152	8·9405		
N × In	48·8812	1	48·8812	5·4674	$0.01 < p < 0.05$
N × A	13·8062	1	13·8062	1·5442	
In × A	1·8062	1	1·8062	0·202	
N × In × A	18·1813	1	14·7452	2·0336	

type of task of forming the impression given $(A_1 \ldots A_5 \ldots N)$, there may be an instruction to remember $A_1 \ldots A_5$. This could explain the observed minimal effect of an explicit instruction *"to remember"* in the *Noun-end* condition.

Figure 2 parallels Fig. 1, showing positional recall of A's in Experiment II when N is given as prompt word. The *Noun-end* curves in the two figures are very similar except for the sudden fall at position 4 in Fig. 2. Also in Fig. 2, the *Noun-first* curve is closer to the *Noun-end* curve. And again, the clear recency effect that was found *for noun-first conditions* in the Louvain study does not show up here.

Table 5 shows the primacy and recency effects for the impression formation data. In this analysis, the difference between the double instruction both to form an impression and to try to remember (Experiment I, Table 2) on the one hand, and the instruction only to form an impression (Experiment II, Table 5) on the other, does not seem to have any effect.

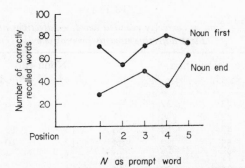

N as prompt word

FIG. 2. Experiment II: Positional recall of adjectives in noun-first and noun-end conditions.

The recall data using the first *A* as prompt word are given in Tables 6, 7 and 8. These results should be compared with the data using *N* as prompt found in Table 3. Total recall, the sum of correct *N*'s and *A*'s is presented in Table 6. It shows that for the *Noun-first* conditions, the recall is about as good when the first *A* is given as prompt word as when *N* is given. A closer inspection of the data, comparing description by description, gives the same outcome. Of 12 possible comparisons (2 conditions × 6 descriptions), five show best recall when *N* is given as prompt word, five show best recall when *A* is given; the last two show no difference at all.

TABLE 5

Results from the impression formation task of Experiment II

Stimulus	Noun-first	Noun-end
Secretary	P	P
Chair	P	R
Movie	R	R
Actress	R	R
Farmer	P	R
Book	P	—

P = Primacy effect
R = Recency effect
— indicates no difference in average rating between A_1–A_5 and A_5–A_1

Observe, however, the results for the *Noun-end* conditions. Here when *A* is given as a prompt, recall is less than half as good as when *N* is the prompt word. And in none of the 12 comparisons does the first *A* give the best recall. Total recall for 20 subjects was only about 40 correct words, which suggests that the task was rather difficult.

TABLE 6

Experiment II: Sum of correctly recalled words—adjectives and nouns.
First adjective used as prompt word

| Stimuli | Noun-first | | | Noun-end | | | |
	A_1–A_5	A_5–A_1	Σ	A_1–A_5	A_5–A_1	Σ	$\Sigma\Sigma$
Actress	22	27	49	4	8	12	61
Movie	22	9	31	1	2	3	34
Farmer	42	14	56	15	10	25	81
Chair	55	29	84	12	10	22	106
Book	17	25	42	5	9	14	56
Secretary	24	20	44	4	5	9	53
	Σ 182	124	306	41	44	85	391

The above analysis may be biased against the *Noun-end* conditions, however. In the *Noun-first* conditions when the first *A* is the prompt word it is at the same time the *A closest* to the *N*; in the *Noun-end* conditions, on the other hand, the first *A* in the description is the *A* furthest away from the *N*. This means that the prompt is an *A* rather closely related to the *N* (as shown in the recall data in Fig. 2) in *Noun-first* condition, but the *A* with the weakest relation of all to the *N* in the *Noun-end* condition. A more "fair" comparison would seem to be between recall data using the *first A* as prompt word in *Noun-first* condition and *last A* as prompt in *Noun-end* condition.

The recall data in Table 6 is a composite measure, and it seems reasonable to split it up and examine how many *N*'s and how many *A*'s are remembered. The results are shown in Tables 7 and 8. Figures 3 and 4 are graphic representations of these results. In Fig. 3, the curve for

TABLE 7

Experiment II: Number of correctly recalled nouns.
First adjective used as prompt word

| Stimuli | Noun-first | | | Noun-end | | | |
	A_1–A_5	A_5–A_1	Σ	A_1–A_5	A_5–A_1	Σ	$\Sigma\Sigma$
Actress	9	11	20	2	4	6	26
Movie	14	6	20	1	0	1	21
Farmer	15	7	22	8	4	12	34
Chair	16	11	27	5	2	7	34
Book	7	12	19	2	4	6	25
Secretary	14	8	22	3	2	5	27
	Σ 75	55	130	21	16	37	167

TABLE 8

Number of correctly recalled adjectives. First adjective used as prompt word.
Experiment II

Position	Noun-first		Noun-end		
	A_1-A_5	A_5-A_1	A_1-A_5	A_5-A_1	Σ
1	35	9	11	6	61
2	30	15	4	11	60
3	19	27	2	6	54
4	23	18	3	5	49
Σ	107	69	20	28	224

Noun-first condition is compared with the *Noun-first curve* from Fig. 2.
Figure 4 shows the corresponding two curves for *Noun-end* conditions.
Figure 3 shows that A's in every position are recalled better when N,
as opposed to the first A, is the prompt word. Giving the first A as
prompt word, however, makes recall of N very high, much higher than
recall of the *first A* when N is given as the prompt. The reverse is true of
recall of the rest of the A's ($A_2 - A_5$), thus making the total recall quite comparable. Figure 3 shows also clearly that the relationship between N and
the first A is not symmetrical. When N is given as prompt, the first A
is correctly recalled 71 times; when the first A is the prompt, N is correctly
recalled 130 times—almost twice as often. In this special case, the back-
ward association is definitely the stronger one!

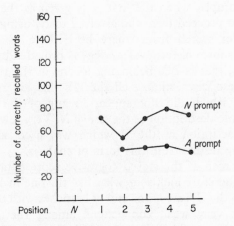

FIG. 3. Experiment II: Positional recall of adjectives and noun. Comparison between
N and A first as prompt words in N-first condition.

The curves for the *Noun-end* condition (Fig. 4) are rather far apart; this might be expected from the poor recall when the first *A* is the prompt word. Notice also that the first *A* is a better prompt for the *N* at the end of the description than for its neighbouring *A*. Both Fig. 3 and Fig. 4 thus show how much easier it is to reproduce the *N* than any of the *A*'s. These results point to the special role of the noun in descriptive phrases.

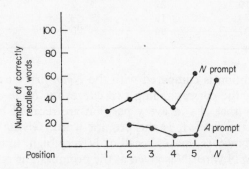

FIG. 4. Experiment II: Positional recall of adjectives and noun. Comparison between *N* and *A* first as prompt words in *N*-end conditions.

This unique nature of the *N*, or perhaps better, this particular structural relationship between the *N* and the *A*'s, can be analysed in somewhat more detail through an inspection of retrieval strategies. What happens, for example, when the first *A* is given as the prompt word? Subjects seem to proceed from the given *A* to *N*, using *N* as a starting point or basis for search from where he tries to "reach" other *A*'s. Evidence for this form of retrieval strategy is provided by persons giving back wrong *N*'s, that is *N*'s belonging to one of the remaining 5 descriptions. In these cases, almost all the *A*'s that are reproduced (disregarding those which did not appear in any of the 6 descriptions) belong to the same description as the *wrong N*. Very few of them belong to the same description as the *A* which was used as prompt word. Table 9 gives the results from this form of analysis.

A topological map of the stored cognitive representation of the description would therefore look somewhat like the one in Fig. 5. The *N* is in the centre and the *A*'s are at the end of branches with different lengths. There are only very weak connections among the *A*'s. Additional evidence for this stems from the poor performance when the first *A* is the prompt word in *Noun-end* conditions (see Table 8). Only one other

TABLE 9

First adjective given as prompt word and an incorrect noun reproduced[a]

	Conditions	A's belonging to noun	A's belonging to prompt word	Other words
Noun-first	A_1–A_5	15	1	12
	A_5–A_1	35	5	48
Noun-end	A_1–A_5	21	3	55
	A_5–A_1	18	4	67
		Σ 89	13	182

[a] The number of the adjectives reproduced belonging to the same description as the wrong noun *versus* the number belonging to the same description as the prompt word.

A out of 24 (4 A's $\times$ 6 descriptions) is correctly reproduced on the average.

Notice, however, that the first A used as prompt word in *Noun-first* condition gives much better recall. This does not necessarily imply stronger connections between A's. It may only reflect a stronger organization of the description in general; that is, it may indicate different

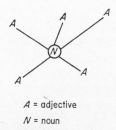

A = adjective

N = noun

FIG. 5. Suggested topological map of stored cognitive representation of noun-adjectives descriptions.

strengths of organization in *Noun-first* and *Noun-end* conditions (see Louvain report), not different types of structure. A stronger organization as such makes the chances for retrieval of correct N much greater and *through this* N the retrieval of other A's from the same description is also made much greater.

REFERENCES

Anderson, N. H. and Norman, Ann (1964). Order effects in impression formation in four classes of stimuli, *J. abnorm. soc. Psychol.* **69,** 467–471.

Rommetveit, R. (1968). "Words, Meanings, and Messages. Theory and Experiments in Psycholinguistics," Academic Press, New York and London.

Word Sequence and Recall

JAN SKJERVE

The research of Wold (1971) and Jaspars *et al.*, 1971 (see pp. 109–138) has given us some information regarding the differential recall of adjectives in *noun + adjectives* versus *adjectives + noun* sequences.

When the *noun* is used as a prompt, the adjectives tend to be recalled better if they are positioned *after* the noun they modify than if they come *before* the noun. These results tend to suggest that the connection between words (adjectives and noun) in decoding is stronger with the adjectives positioned after the noun than the opposite sequence, adjectives-noun.

In Norwegian and French, the position of adjective and noun differs in phrases consisting of one noun, one or more adjectives plus articles and conjunctions. The structure of the grammar requires that the adjective be positioned before the noun in Norwegian, unless as in Wold's study (pp. 127–138) a relative clause is used; in French, on the other hand, one tends to find the opposite sequence, noun followed by adjectives. If it is the case as suggested above that, independent of the structure of a given language, the noun and adjective connection is stronger in noun-adjective sequences than in adjective-noun sequences when decoding is involved, it is hypothesized that Frenchmen recalling French phrases will do better than Norwegians recalling equivalent Norwegian phrases. It is, also, hypothesized that as Norwegian is an adjective-noun language there will be more adjectives displaced and recalled with the wrong noun than in French.

METHOD

Subjects

The subjects were 9 Norwegian and 9 French students; both groups consisted of five girls and four boys.

Stimulus Material

In the selection of the stimulus material, an attempt was made to use Norwegian and French words which corresponded as closely as possible in terms of meaning and frequency. Frequency was judged intuitively, not by consulting frequency lists. A total of 17 Norwegian-French phrases were constructed, each of which consisted of one noun plus one or more adjectives plus conjunctions and articles. In addition, there was one list of 15 adjectives in both French and Norwegian versions; none of the adjectives which occurred on this pure adjective list was used in any of the phrases. The stimulus phrases are presented in Table 1 with their English translations.

TABLE 1

Stimulus phrases

English	Norwegian	French
1. A new and white car	en ny og hvit bil	une voiture nouvelle et blanche
2. An African elephant	en afrikansk elefant	un éléphant africain
3. A coquettish and charming girl	en kokett og sjarmerende pike	une fille coquette et charmante
4. White teeth	hvite tanner	des dents blanches
5. A dull, tottering and sallow seventy-year-old	en sløv vaklende og gusten syttiåring	un septuagénaire hébété, vacillant et blafard
6. Narrow and dark streets	trange og mørke gater	des rues étroites et sombres
7. The red book	den røde boken	le livre rouge
8. A pear-shaped and protruding stomach	en pæreformet og framstående mage	un ventre piriforme et proéminent
9. Political and religious freedom	politisk og religiøs frihet	la liberté politique et religieuse
10. Naïve eyes	naive øyne	des yeux naïfs
11. A narrow-minded, false and abominable character	en smålig, falsk og avskyelig karakter	une nature mesquine, fausse et exécrable
12. A blue orange	en blå appelsin	une orange bleue
13. An expensive and attractive commodity	en dyr og tiltrekkende vare	une marchandise chère et attirante
14. A green and lonely house	et grønt og ensomt hus	une maison verte et solitaire
15. Dark hair	mørkt hår	des cheveux foncés
16. An unstable and contradictory opinion	en ustabil og motstridende opinion	une opinion instable et contradictoire
17. A big, spotted and dirty dog	en stor flekkete og skitten hund	un chien grand, taché et sale

Procedure

The subjects were presented first with the pure adjective list. The list was read aloud and subjects were instructed to remember the words and to write them down as soon as the reading of the list was finished. Next the phrases were read aloud to the subjects. They were read as if the entire set of phrases was one continuous text, without using distinct pauses between items. The instructions were the same as those used for the recall of the list of adjectives. The subjects wrote down what they remembered on special answer sheets. These sheets were not handed out until the reading of the phrases was completed. On the answer sheets the phrases minus the adjectives were printed; for example,

"A . . . and . . . car."

These phrase skeletons or prompts were randomized on the answer sheets so that their order did not correspond to the order of the stimulus presentation.

RESULTS AND DISCUSSION

The results for recall of the list of adjectives alone are shown in Table 2, part 1; the results of prompted phrase recall are shown in Table 2, part 2. The difference between French and Norwegian groups

TABLE 2

Recall by the Norwegian and the French groups

			Total number recalled	Mean	Range	t	Level of significance
1.	Recall test	Nor.	72	8	6–10	—	—
		Fre.	74	8·2	7–10		
2.	Recall of	Nor.	83	9·2	5–17	2·56	$0·02 > p > 0·01$
	phrases	Fre.	135	15	9–27		
3.	Displace-	Nor.	12	1·33	1–2	1·72	$0·06 > p > 0·05$
	ment	Fre.	7	0·78	0–2		

on word list recall is negligible. However, on the recall of phrases the French group did significantly better than the Norwegian group ($t = 2·56$, $p < 0·02$) and the French group also made fewer displacements ($t = 1·72$, $p < 0·06$), i.e. they made fewer errors in which they connected an adjective up with the wrong noun on the answer sheet.

The present study differs from the earlier works of Jaspars *et al.*, 1971 (pp. 109–125) and Wold, 1971 (pp. 127–138) in that in these latter two studies, the first part of the subject's task was to form an impression, then secondly the subject was asked to recall the stimuli; in the present study, the experimental task was one of pure recall. Also the phrases used in the present study were more natural than those used in the earlier experiments, in the sense that they are more likely to occur in everyday language. But as the hypothesis was confirmed in the present experiment, there is some evidence that there is something special about the sequence noun-adjective in language processing. The findings of this short experiment give us some information regarding how different structures of language facilitate memory.

REFERENCES

Jaspars, J., Rommetveit, R., Cook, M., Havelka, N., Henry, P., Herkner, W., Pêcheux, M. and Peeters, G. (1971). Order effects in impression formation. *In* "Social Contexts of Messages" (E. A. Carswell and R. Rommetveit, eds), pp. 109–125. Academic Press, London and New York.
Wold, A. H. (1971). Impression formation: A psycholinguistic approach. *In* "Social Contexts of Messages" (E. A. Carswell and R. Rommetveit, eds), pp. 127–138. Academic Press, London and New York.

The Temporal Perspective of Remembering[a]

STEINAR KVALE

George Orwell in his novel "1984" emphasized "the mutability of the past" and described in detail how a nation's past is changed when "history is continually rewritten (1949)". G. H. Mead has described how the past reaches us only through our present "frames of reference or perspectives (1932)". Starting with spatial perspective, Graumann (1960) has discussed phenomenological and empirical evidence for the general perspective nature of cognitive processes. Husserl, who undertook a phenomenological elaboration of James's "stream of consciousness", concluded that "memory is in a continual flux" through an "*a priori* necessary retroaction (1928)". An example of a tendency for the meaning of the past to change when seen in the new context of the present is the Munich Treaty; originally in 1938 it was hailed as a victory for peace, but with the outbreak of the Second World War it came to be regarded as a disastrous political blunder.

The present paper deals with this issue, whether the memory of an event may be retroactively determined by the context and perspective in which it is remembered. From a psychological point of view, a meaning organization of memory (e.g. Broadbent, 1966) would not contradict a process of continual memory change as a result of meaning's dependence upon context. If the meaning of an event is what is remembered (decoding), and this meaning is changed by the succeeding context, *meaning retroaction* (recoding), the event as recalled may have been changed (encoding). This suggests a temporal perspective for remembering; how an event is remembered may depend upon the context succeeding it. It is possible that not only the *meaning* of an event, but also the *form* of the event as remembered, may be changed by its succeeding context. Thus a *meaning retroaction* hypothesis for remembering contrasts with the assumption of some kind of immutable memory traces implied by the "permanent memory hypothesis" ("the permanent

[a] This is a progress report of a study supported by Norges almenvitenskapelige forskningsråd and the Alexander von Humboldt-Stiftung.

record of the stream of consciousness" in Penfield's expression) which is implicit in several psychological theories of memory (Adams, 1967).

The meaning retroaction hypothesis for remembering is based on three assumptions:

1. The meaning of an event is what is remembered.

2. The meaning of an ambiguous event can be retroactively changed by the context succeeding it.

3. The meaning of an event may be expressed by several synonymous forms.

The hypothesis then states that the form of a reproduced event can be altered in the direction of the meaning given retroactively by the succeeding context.

Although there have been several studies of the influence of proactive sets on the perception or memory of an event within the psycholinguistic tradition (e.g. Miller and Selfridge, 1953; Howes and Osgood, 1954), investigation of the influence of retroactive sets resulting from the succeeding context of an event have been rare (for one exception see Rommetveit and Turner, 1967). Carmichael *et al.* (1932) conducted a "proactive experiment", the results of which showed that a name (Determining Stimulus) preceding a visual figure (Original Stimulus), affects the reproduction of the figure. Graham (1951), among others, interpreted these results as evidence of a "perceptual change" rather than a "memory change". However, the results of the Hanawalt and Demarest (1939) experiment, in which names were given some time after the figures were presented, and just before reproduction, may only be interpreted as interfering with remembering. These experimental results may, however, partly be due to a stronger recency effect of the names as compared with figures at the time of reproduction.

Prentice (1954) has suggested that the distorted reproductions found in the experiment by Carmichael *et al.* (1932) might merely have been caused by interference with the drawing behaviour of reproduction rather than by memory change itself. Prentice tested this hypothesis by using a recognition task in place of the original reproduction task; Prentice's hypothesis was supported as no evidence of memory change was found when the recognition test was used.

In this paper two separate experiments dealing with the influence of meaning retroaction upon remembering are reported; one involves ambiguous figures (see Fig. 1) and the other ambiguous words (see Fig. 2). In both experiments ambiguous and synonymous mediation (Heider, 1958) were employed within a retroactive interference paradigm. An ambiguous stimulus (Original Stimulus) was presented and then the meaning was determined in two different ways by differing succeeding contexts (Interfering stimuli, hereafter referred to as Determining Stimulus A or B). In reproduction the two different retroactively determined meanings of the originally ambiguous stimulus may be expressed by a copy of the Original Stimulus, or by several synonymous forms, which differ for the A or B determined meaning. Two matched groups of subjects were presented with the same Original Stimulus, but with different succeeding Determining Stimuli; one group was given Determining Stimulus A and the other Determining Stimulus B. According to the meaning-retroaction hypothesis of remembering it was predicted that the Original Stimulus would tend to be reproduced differently in the two groups.

The present experimental design deviates form traditional retroactive interference studies of memory in two major respects. First, it does not focus upon the quantitative amount of the Original Stimulus retained, but upon qualitative changes of the Original Stimulus as a result of retroactive interference. Second, the Original and Determining Stimuli are not isolated, unrelated items, but stand in a contextual relation to each other, the relation being that of retroactive meaning determination of the Original Stimulus by the Determining Stimulus.

EXPERIMENT I: REMEMBERING OF FIGURES
METHOD

Subjects

The subjects were pupils of high schools in Heidelberg; they were 16–18 years old and of both sexes. The experiments were conducted entirely in the German language.

Experimental Design

A modification of a design developed by Carmichael *et al.* (1932) was used. The present design is shown in Fig. 1. Here an ambiguous figure which may mean either a pear or a bottle is depicted. This same Original Stimulus (*OS*) was presented to matched *A* and *B* subgroups, who were told that reproduction would be asked for. After presentation of *OS* terminated, the *A* subgroup heard the sentence "The last figure was a pear", which was the Determining Stimulus (*DS*) that retroactively determined the ambiguous figure to mean a pear. After the same *OS* was presented to the *B* subgroup it was retroactively determined to be a bottle

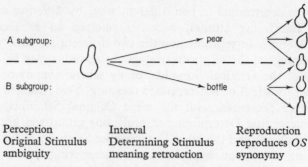

Perception	Interval	Reproduction
Original Stimulus	Determining Stimulus	reproduces *OS*
ambiguity	meaning retroaction	synonymy

FIG. 1. Experimental design of figure experiment.

in the manner just described. The two different retroactively determined meanings may be correctly depicted by the *OS* figure or by synonymous figures, which will tend to be different for the *A* and *B* meanings (see Fig. 1.

In each of the conditions in the present experiment 12 ambiguous figures were presented for 2 seconds each before a test of memory of the 12 figures was called for. Within each of the experimental conditions, the *A* subgroup was given the 12 *A*-names to the 12 figures and the *B* subgroup was given the 12 *B*-names to the same 12 figures.

In addition to the *A* and *B* subgroup conditions, there were three conditions representing different temporal relations between *OS* and *DS*. In the *Retroactive Condition* (depicted in Fig. 1) each figure (*OS*) was immediately succeeded by a name (*DS*) defining the meaning of the ambiguous figure. In the *Suggestion Condition* (used by Hanawalt and Demarest, 1939) the names (*DS*) were withheld until immediately before reproduction of each figure. In the *Proactive Condition* (employed by Carmichael *et al.*, 1932) the names (*DS*) defining the figures immediately preceded the presentation of each figure (*OS*). In the *Control Condition* no names accompanied the figures, either at the time of original presentation or at the time of reproduction.

Memory for *OS* was measured both by reproduction and recognition tests. "Exact" reproduction of the figures was called for at three different time intervals: immediately after presentation of the last of the 12 figures (Short term memory, STM),[a] 20 minutes after presentation (Medium term memory, MTM), and two days after presentation (Long term memory, LTM). The use of the recognition test was limited to the STM and MTM conditions. Different subjects served for each time interval and for each test. After the subjects had reproduced or recog-

---

[a] The term STM as used here is an extension of the common usage found in the literature, i.e. meaning intervals of a few seconds.

nized the figures, they were asked for their own conceptions of what the figures represented.

The subjects' reproductions were scored by two judges. They did not know whether a given reproduction came from the A or B subgroup. The response categories scored for reproduction were (1) A-name distortion, (2) B-name distortion, (3) other distortions, and (4) no distortion. For each of the 12 stimulus figures the recognition test contained three items: (1) a copy of the original figure, (2) a figure slightly distorted towards the A-name, and (3) a figure slightly distorted towards the B-name.

In a pretest, an attempt was made to determine the degree of ambiguity of the 12 stimulus items. The pretest subjects were not asked to reproduce the figures but instead were presented with the figures and asked to state their own conceptions of what the 12 figures represented. The names given by subjects showed large variations in the degree of ambiguity of the 12 figures. For some figures, the A and B meanings were about equally often reported, whereas for other figures, one of the meanings tended to dominate almost entirely. It was hypothesized that the experimental results would show meaning retroaction influencing reproduction/recognition both of the ambiguous figures and of the relatively unequivocal figures.

RESULTS AND DISCUSSION

In general the results tended to support the hypothesis that meaning retroaction may influence the reproduction of visual figures. Of the 480 possible reproductions in the *Retroaction* and *Suggestion, STM* and *MTM, Conditions* (4 conditions $\times$ 10 subjects $\times$ 12 figures), 346 were reproduced. Of these no drawing was scored by the two judges as an instance of "non-distortion"; and 70 were scored as miscellaneous "other distortions". The remaining 276 reproductions were distributed between A-name distortions and B-name distortions as shown in Table 1a. The A subgroup of subjects showed 101 A-type distortions and only 33 B-type distortions; similarly, the B-subgroup showed 95 B-type

TABLE 1a

Meaning retroactive reproductions of ambiguous figures (OS)
(Retro STM, MTM and Sug STM, MTM combined)

	A distortions	B distortions
A subgroups $(DS = A)$ $(Ss : 20)$	101	33
B subgroups $(DS = B)$ $(Ss : 20)$	46	95

distortions and 46 *A*-type distortions. Thus these results do suggest that subjects' reproductions of ambiguous figures tend to be distorted in the direction of the succeeding, determining context.

The results of the recognition task were not as strong as those of the reproduction task. Of the 984 recognition choices, almost half (464) were of the copies of *OS*. The distribution of the remaining 520 choices gives less evidence for the influence of meaning retroaction (see Table 1b). However, support for the meaning retroaction hypothesis is strengthened by the finding that not only ambiguous figures, but also those figures which were shown by pretest to be relatively unequivocal were influenced by meaning retroaction when reproduced.

TABLE 1b

Meaning retroactive recognition of ambiguous figures (OS)
(Retro STM, MTM and Sug STM combined)

	A distorted	*B* distorted
A subgroups (*DS* = *A*) (*Ss* : 41)	140	128
B subgroups (*DS* = *B*) (*Ss* : 41)	97	155

The results for the different temporal conditions are analysed separately in Table 2a (*reproduction*) and Table 2b (*recognition*). The numbers in Table 2a show the percentage of reproductions distorted towards names given minus the percentage of reproductions distorted towards the "opposite" names (which were *NOT* given) within each temporal condition. In addition to the conditions included in Table 1a, a *Retroactive LTM* and a *Proactive STM condition* are included in Table 2a.

Table 2a shows that the names given immediately after presentation of the figures (*Retroaction condition*) influenced reproduction whether it occurred at 1-minute (STM), 20-minute (MTM), or 2-day intervals (LTM) after the presentation of the 12 figures and names. In the *Suggestion Condition*, when no names accompanied the presentation of the figures and when the names were first given immediately prior to reproduction of each figure, the names again tended to influence reproduction whether the figures had been presented a few minutes before (STM) or 20 minutes before (MTM). Thus it might be that meaning retroaction may influence reproduction independently of the time interval between presentation of the *OS* and reproduction. Although several recent studies have reported an increased importance of a meaning organization of memory from short term memory to long term memory (Baddeley and

TABLE 2a

Meaning influenced reproduction of ambiguous figures (OS)
Temporal conditions (*A and B subgroups combined*)

Sequence OS–DS:	Interval OS–Reproduction:					
	Ss	STM	Ss	MTM	Ss	LTM
Retro: OS–DS . . . Rep OS	(10)	35%	(10)	28%	(28)	43%
Sug: OS . . . . . . DS–Rep OS	(10)	42%	(10)	30%		
Pro: DS–OS . . . Rep OS	(10)	39%				

TABLE 2b

Meaning influenced recognition of ambiguous figures (OS)
Temporal conditions (*A and B subgroups combined*)

	Ss	STM	Ss	MTM
Retro	(32)	8%	(32)	12%
Sug	(18)	1%		

Dale, 1966), the hypothesis that the influence of meaning retroaction upon remembering would increase from STM to MTM to LTM was not confirmed in the present experiment.

Table 2a also shows that meaning retroaction may influence reproduction of figures independently of the time interval between figures (*OS*) and defining names (*DS*) which varies from a few seconds (all *Retroactive Conditions*) to a few minutes (*Suggestion Condition, STM*) to more than 20 minutes (*Suggestion Condition, MTM*). The results of the investigation of the effects of temporal relations show that meaning retroaction tended to influence reproduction regardless of the length of time between *OS* presentation and *DS*.

The results of the *Proactive Condition* in the present experiment replicated those of Carmichael *et al.* (1932) in that the preceding context affected the form in which the stimulus was reproduced; also, the present experiment replicates the Hanawalt and Demarest (1939) experiment, showing that *DS* presented at the time of reproduction affected the form of the items recalled. In addition, the results of the *Retroactive Condition* of the present experiment show that the presentation of *DS* immediately after the presentation of *OS* affects reproduction. This is a new finding.

As is the case with the findings of the Hanawalt and Demarest (1939) experiment, the findings in the *Suggestion Condition* in the present experiment are not easily reconciled with the common interpretation of the *Proactive Condition* that the changed reproductions found are due to "perceptual change" or "a distorted perception" (e.g. Graham, 1951; Hilgard and Atkinson, 1967). As the presentation of the figures had terminated when the names were given, one would have to expand the concept of perception to cover "postpresentation perceptual processes" (Aaronson, 1967), in order to interpret the findings in our *Retroactive Condition* as perceptual changes rather than as memory changes.

Table 2b shows the percentage of recognition choices distorted towards the names given, minus the number of recognition choices of figures distorted towards the opposite names which were not given, within each temporal condition. It is evident from this table that the influence of meaning retroaction upon recognition is limited to the *Retroactive Condition*. This very slight tendency might suggest that Prentice's (1954) interpretation of distorted figure reproductions as merely caused by interference with drawing skill cannot entirely account for the present results. In some way the remembered form of the figures appears to be influenced by meaning retroaction.

Investigation of the subjects' spontaneous conceptions of the figures revealed that the types of subjects' conceptions reported following the experimental testing generally corresponded to the conceptions reported by a pretest group who had no reproduction condition. The effects of the subjects' own conceptions upon reproduction were investigated separately in the *Control Condition*. In this condition when no names accompanied the stimulus figures, either at the time of *OS* presentation or at the time of reproduction, the distortive influence of subjects' own conceptions upon reproduction about equalled the influence of the experimenter's definitions in the experimental conditions. The subjects' own conceptions of the figures which were opposed to the experimenter's definition may partly explain the reproductions and recognitions distorted towards the names not given (see Tables 1a and 1b).

It would seem that three main types of relationship may be said to exist between a *subject's* own immediate conception of a figure and the *experimenter's* retroactive definition of the figure:

1. *Retroactive attribution:* no own conception; conception determined by retroactive meaning given by determining stimulus.

2. *Retroactive confirmation:* own conception is reinforced by determining stimulus.

3. *Retroactive disconfirmation:* own conception is contradicted by determining stimulus.

In the *Retroactive* and *Suggestion Conditions*, the subjects retrospectively reported they had had their own conceptions of the figures *before* they heard the experimenter's definitions for about half of the reproduced figures. Separate analyses showed that the names retroactively given by the experimenter influenced the subjects' reproductions when no conceptions of their own were reported (retroactive attribution) as well as when the experimenter's name was opposite to the subject's own conception of the figure (retroactive disconfirmation or change). For example the subject's own conception might be "pear" and the experimenter's definition might be "bottle".

It may be argued that the present experiment does not show any very conclusive evidence of the influence of meaning retroaction upon the remembering of figures. It is possible that a subject may have entirely forgotten the *OS* presented and merely drawn a new "synonymous" figure according to a remembered name (*Retroactive Condition*) or a given name (*Suggestion Condition*). Two findings suggest that this cannot entirely account for the results. First, when the subjects were asked, they stated that almost half of their drawings had not been influenced by the experimenter's definitions at all. Second, a name drawing test was devised to check how subjects would normally represent the names or labels used in the experiment. Two groups of subjects who had not seen the original figures were asked to draw the figures are only hearing the 12 *A* or 12 *B* names. These "synonymous" drawings differed markedly from the drawings reproduced in the experimental conditions. Although some reproductions may have been drawn only from a name remembered or given, this can hardly have occurred for the majority of reproductions.

EXPERIMENT II. REMEMBERING OF WORDS IN SENTENCES
METHOD

Subjects

The population of subjects was the same as that described in Experiment I.

Experimental Design

In the sentence experiment the same ambiguous word (*OS*) was presented in different sentence contexts (*DS*) to matched *A* and *B* subgroups, who knew that reproduction would be asked for. Figure 2 shows the ambiguous word "illuminate" which in isolation may mean abstractly "to explain", or more literally "to light up". To *A* subgroup, "illuminate" was retroactively defined in the more abstract way as it was heard in the following sentence: "*To illuminate (OS) this better, I shall give yet another example (DS)*" ("Um die Sache besser zu beleuchten

(*OS*), gebe ich noch ein weiteres Beispiel (*DS*)"); to *B* subgroup "illuminate" was retroactively defined in the more literal way in the *B* version of the sentence: "*To illuminate (OS) this better, I shall find a better lamp (DS) for you*" ("Um die Sache besser zu beleuchten (*OS*), hole ich eine bessere Lampe (*DS*) für Sie").

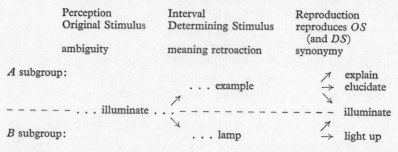

A sentence: "To illuminate (*OS*) this better, I shall give yet another example (*DS*)."
B sentence: "To illuminate (*OS*) this better, I shall find another lamp (*DS*) for you."

Fig. 2. Experimental design of sentence experiment.

The time interval between the original ambiguous word (*OS*) and the main determining word (*DS*) varied in the 10 sentences from half a second (1 syllable) to 10 seconds (36 syllables). Memory of the ambiguous word was measured by both reproduction and recognition tests and at two different time intervals. Five sentences were read together as a group before reproduction of the sentences "as verbatim as possible" was called for. In the STM condition, reproduction followed immediately after the fifth sentence with about one minute delay for instructions. In the LTM condition, reproduction was first asked for after 3 days. For each time interval different groups of subjects were used. But in contrast to the figure experiments, the same subjects were given the reproduction and recognition tests.

The subjects in the STM condition first heard five sentences and then were given reproduction and recognition tasks. Thereafter, the same subjects heard the last five of the ten sentences, which were again followed by reproduction and recognition tasks. In the LTM condition each subject only heard five sentences in all, either the first five or the last five, which were followed by reproduction and recognition tasks.

The recognition task was given to the subjects after they had written down the sentences they remembered. Each recognition item consisted of the complete original sentence with two synonyms in addition to the ambiguous word; for example,

(clarify)
"To (explain)   this better, I shall give yet another example"—
(illuminate)
(*A* version).

As both the additional synonyms corresponded to only one of the possible interpretations (*A* or *B* meanings) and different versions of the recognition task were given in the *A* and *B* subgroups, the results of the recognition task are not relevant to the issue of meaning retroaction and remembering. The recognition test is, however, relevant to the issue of an increased meaning-organization of memory from STM to LTM.

In the sentences used for the memory tasks there was a meaningful contextual relation between the ambiguous word (*OS*) and the determining word (*DS*). As a separate experimental condition (*Word List Condition*), the words of five sentences were scrambled in a random order, but *OS* and *DS* retained their relative position within each sentence. These word lists were read to a group of subjects in the same way as the sentences, and immediate reproduction was asked for (*STM*).

The degree of ambiguity of *OS* was tested in a pretest by using a sentence completion test. In this test, subjects were asked to complete a sentence following the ambiguous word (e.g. "*To illuminate* . . ."). The completions of the ten sentences showed large variations in the degree of "ambiguity of the ambiguous word". It varied from about half *A* meaning and half *B* meaning of some ambiguous words to almost entirely one meaning for other words. As in the case of the figure experiment, it was hypothesized that not only the reproduction of the ambiguous words (*OS*), but also the reproduction of the fairly unequivocal *OS* would be retroactively influenced by the succeeding context.

RESULTS AND DISCUSSION

On the whole the results of the sentence experiment showed stronger support for the influence of meaning retroaction in reproduction than was found in the figure experiment. In the sentence experiment, there were a total of 720 possible reproductions of the ambiguous word in the *Retroactive STM and LTM Conditions* (40 subjects $\times$ 10 sentences + 64 subjects $\times$ 5 sentences). A total of 472 reproductions of the ambiguous word (*OS*) occurred. Of these, 354 were scored by the two judges as verbatim reproductions and 10 as miscellaneous other reproductions, not corresponding to either the *A* or *B* meaning of the ambiguous word. The remaining 108 reproductions were scored as *A* and *B* synonyms of the ambiguous word. Table 3 shows that 58 out of 59 *A* synonyms were given by *A* subgroup and all 49 *B* synonyms were given by the *B* subgroup.

It is evident that when the ambiguous words were not reproduced verbatim but were replaced by synonyms, these synonyms were entirely different in the *A* and *B* subgroups. Also, not only relatively ambiguous words, but also fairly unequivocal "ambiguous" words were replaced by synonyms on reproduction in correspondence with the meaning given retroactively at the time of reproduction. Thus the results suggest

TABLE 3

Meaning retroactive synonymous reproductions of ambiguous words (OS)
(Retro STM and LTM combined)

	A meaning	*B* meaning
A subgroups (*DS = A*) (*Ss* : 52)	58	0
B subgroups (*DS = B*) (*Ss* : 52)	1	49

that words heard after the original ambiguous word may influence how it is reproduced.

In Table 4 the results of the *A* and *B* subgroups within each experimental condition have been combined. The numbers in Table 4 show the percentage of reproductions/recognitions of the ambiguous word falling into each of the four categories: Verbatim, Synonymous (*A* or *B* meaning), Miscellaneous, Omitted.

Meaning retroactive reproductions occurred with immediate reproduction (STM) as well as with reproduction delayed until three days after presentation (LTM). Table 4 shows an increased ratio of synonymous reproductions to verbatim reproductions from STM (13%/64%) to LTM (17%/31%). This indicates that the influence of meaning retroaction increases with time before reproduction. The relative increase of synonymous reproductions and recognitions from STM to LTM is in line with other studies reporting an increased importance of a meaning organization from STM to LTM (Baddeley and Dale, 1966).

From Table 4 it is also evident that in the *Word List Condition* synonymous reproductions of the ambiguous word were practically eliminated. The influence of meaning retroaction upon reproduction appears largely confined to a meaningful contextual relation between ambiguous and determining stimuli.

TABLE 4

Reproduction and recognition of ambiguous words (OS)
Temporal conditions (A *and* B *subgroups combined*) *and Word List*

| | STM | | | | LTM | | | | |
	Ss	Verb	Syn	Misc	Om	Ss	Verb	Syn	Misc	Om
Retro Sentences Repro	(40)	64%	13%	1%	22%	(64)	31%	17%	2%	50%
Retro Sentences Recog	(40)	89%	11%	—	—	(64)	76%	24%	—	—
Retro Word lists Repro	(38)	17%	1%	1%	81%					

Meaning retroactive reproductions occurred with all time intervals between *OS* and *DS*, and thus also when the time interval exceeded the "perceived present" of about 5 seconds and the normal memory span of about 25 syllables in a sentence (Fraisse, 1963). Again it would seem necessary to postulate "postpresentational perceptual processes" in order to interpret the present findings as evidence of perceptual change rather than of memory change.

It may be argued that subjects, listening to the sentence, postpone giving meaning to the ambiguous word until the determining words have been heard. A detailed subject description given in a pilot test shows some evidence for this:

"Attempted mainly to get the meaning of the sentence, and secondly the exact word form . . . Must hear the sentence to an end, during the reading little was noticed. Mostly the whole sense and meaning, and tried to attend to it globally, to notice it looking backwards. During the reading the words do not say much, I wait for that which follows . . . There the whole sentence was necessary, the (words) . . . could first obtain a meaning at the end, be seen as a whole."

Such a "post-integration or delayed coding process" has been discussed by Rommetveit and Turner (1967). If this were the general case, the present findings of meaning retroaction influencing reproduction would be limited to retroactive attribution (delayed encoding). The experimental findings then could not be interpreted as evidence of retroactive disconfirmation (recoding) influencing reproduction, leading to changes in the past as remembered.

As a check of this possibility, the sentences were read to a separate group of subjects who were not asked to reproduce the sentences. After each sentence they were asked whether the ambiguous word had changed its meaning as they listened to the sentence to the end. For about 1/4 of the sentences, subjects reported experiencing a change of the ambiguous word's meaning as they heard its succeeding context. This suggests that not only retroactive attribution (delayed encoding), but also retroactive disconfirmation (recoding) of the ambiguous words may have influenced its reproduction in the present experiment.

As in the case of the figure experiment another possible interpretation of the experimental findings might be that subjects had entirely forgotten the ambiguous word's form and meaning, but remembered the more salient determining word(s) at the end of the sentences from which they reconstructed some equally probable word in place of the ambiguous word. Such a reconstructive process of reproduction was partly described by the subject quoted previously:

"The beginning of the sentence mostly still in word form, and in the middle very uncertain, and tried to get on with my own words, because I still had the meaning present, tried to fill in the correct meaning . . . If it was 'elucidate' (erleuchten) or 'illuminate' (beleuchten) or 'explain' (erklären) I do not know any more. But 'to give an example' I still knew, and that 'an example' is mostly 'explained'. Selected the most common."

The general meaning of the ambiguous word is remembered and the exact word form of the determining word; then the most probable form of the ambiguous word is selected from among several synonyms.

Two findings are contrary to pure reconstruction from the determining word being the general way of reproducing the ambiguous word. First, when asked, the subjects generally could tell whether the ambiguous word had been reproduced verbatim or not. Second, two measures of contextual determination of the ambiguous word were given to separate groups. The first task involved the insertion of the stimulus word; for each of the sentences the preceding and succeeding context of the ambiguous word was given and the subjects' task was to insert the appropriate missing word (OS) (e.g. "To . . . this better, I shall give yet another example"). The second task was one of multiple selection. Here the complete sentences were given, but with two synonyms added to the ambiguous word. The subjects' task was to select the most appropriate of the three multiple selection alternatives (same sentence form as in recognition test). The two measures of context determination contained fewer verbatim insertions of the original ambiguous words than occurred in the reproduced/recognized sentences. This suggests that the ambiguous words generally were remembered and not merely reconstructed from the more salient determining words in the succeeding context.

CONCLUSION

The succeeding context of an event may retroactively determine the meaning of the event. The two separate, but formally similar, experiments described above have shown that such a meaning retroaction may influence reproduction of both figures and words in sentences. A slight effect of meaning retroaction upon recognition of figures was also found. Meaning retroaction influenced reproduction of ambiguous as well as fairly unequivocal figures and words.

Meaning retroaction was found to influence reproduction of figures and of words with several different time intervals between presentation of OS and reproduction, and with a variety of temporal relations between OS and DS. The findings suggested that not merely perceptual changes, but also memory changes had occurred.

Retroactive attribution (delayed encoding) as well as retroactive disconfirmation (recoding) of the OS was found to influence reproduction. The contextual interpretation of the changed reproductions of the OS being due only to guessing from the more salient DS was not found to be probable.

The present experimental findings might be interpreted as suggesting that not only the meaning, but also the form of the past as remembered, may be continuously altered. The notion of some kind of immutable "memory traces" appears difficult to reconcile with the present findings, which give empirical support to the conception of memory in a continual flux through meaning retroaction.

A reinterpretation of "simple facts" may lead to a change in the facts as remembered. The "permanent memory hypothesis" should perhaps be replaced by the conception of a temporal perspective of remembering. How an event is remembered may depend upon the temporal context and perspective in which it is remembered. For the psychology of memory it then becomes an important theoretical and practical task to investigate systematically the mutability versus fixedness of memory in terms of which events are remembered, and the situations in which perceiving and remembering occurs. Such investigations might have implications for the psychology of testimony and for the study of history.

REFERENCES

Aaronson, D. (1967). Temporal factors in perception and short-term memory, *Psychol. Bull.* **67**, 130–144.

Adams, J. A. (1967). "Human Memory," McGraw-Hill, New York.

Baddeley, A. D. and Dale, H. G. (1966). The effect of semantic similarity on retroactive interference in long- and short-term memory, *J. verbal Learn. verbal Behav.* **5**, 417–420.

Broadbent, D. E. (1966). Recent analyses of short-term memory. *In* "Symposium 21: Short-term and Long-term Memory" (Broadbent, D. E., ed.), pp. 18–25. International Congress of Psychology, Moscow.

Carmichael, L., Hogan, P. H. and Walter, A. A. (1932). An experimental study of the effect of language on the reproduction of visually perceived form, *J. exp. Psychol.* **15**, 73–86.

Fraisse, P. (1963). "The Psychology of Time," Harper & Row, New York.

Graham, C. H. (1951). Visual perception. *In* "Handbook of Experimental Psychology" (Stevens, S. S., ed.), pp. 868–916. John Wiley, New York.

Graumann, C. F. (1960). "Grundlagen einer Phänomenologie und Psychologie der Perspektivität," de Gruyter, Berlin.

Hanawalt, N. G. and Demarest, I. H. (1939). The effect of verbal suggestion in the recall period upon the reproduction of visually perceived forms, *J. exp. Psychol.* **25**, 159–174.

Heider, F. (1958). "The Psychology of Interpersonal Relations," John Wiley, New York.

Hilgard, E. R. and Atkinson, R. C. (1967). "Introduction to Psychology," Harcourt, Brace & World, New York.

Howes, D. and Osgood, C. E. (1954). On the combination of associative probabilities in linguistic contexts, *Am. J. Psychol.* **67**, 241–258.

Husserl, E. (1964). "The Phenomenology of Internal Time Consciousness," Nijhoff, The Hague.

Mead, G. H. (1932). "The Philosophy of the Present," Open Court, La Salle Illinois.

Miller, G. A. and Selfridge, J. A. (1953). Verbal context and the recall of meaningful material, *Am. J. Psychol.* **63**, 176–185.

Orwell, G. (1949). "1984," Secker & Warburg, London.

Prentice, W. C. H. (1954). Visual recognition of verbally labeled figures, *Am. J. Psychol.* **67**, 315–320.

Rommetveit, R. and Turner, E. A. (1967). A study of "chunking" in transmission of messages, *Lingua* **18**, 337–351.

AUTHOR INDEX

Numbers in italic refer to the pages on which the reference appears.

159

SUBJECT INDEX

Addressee, 67, 77–80, 83, 86, 88–92
Adjective, noun order, 10, 11, 30, 109–123, 127–137, 139–142
Affective meaning, 13, 19, 20, 22, 98, 104
Ambiguity, 6, 21, 23, 24, 34, 144–157
Apparent shifting, 79, 80, 83, 84, 88, 89
Apposition, 124
Ascending adjective order, 112, 114–119, 121, 129
Assertion, 86, 87, 92, 94
Associative meaning, 19, 20, 22–24
Attributes, 97–104, 111–124, 126–137, 139–142
Attribution,
  sender, 97–102
  theory, 10, 97, 98, 101

Binocular rivalry, 15–17

Cognitive, perceptual operations, 14–25
Cognitive representations, 14–25, 136, 137
Communication,
  channel, 77
  process, 3–10, 14, 29, 30, 77–79, 88, 94
  setting, 3–10, 13–15, 18–21, 25, 29, 30, 32–34, 52–55, 77–95
Compatibility, 98–104
Competence, 4, 85
Comprehension, 16, 18, 22–24, 30, 34–36
Conditions of,
  interpretation, 81–83, 91–93
  production, 82–85, 89, 92, 93
Conflict situations, 81
Congruity, 16
Connotative meaning, 78, 80, 83

Consistency, 97
Constituents, 97
Constraints, situational, 80
Content clue, 36–55, 57–65
Content elements, 31–55, 57, 58, 71, 72
Content words, 19–22, 35, 40
Context, 5–8, 14, 18–24, 29, 33–55, 77–79, 94, 143, 144
  determining, 144–157
  extralinguistic, 3–10, 24
  intralinguistic, 9–11, 24, 109–124
  linguistic, 8, 23, 24, 29, 30
  non-appropriate, 32, 33, 37, 41, 44–55, 59–61
  non-linguistic, 3–11, 29–55, 124
  picture, 10, 36, 37, 40–55, 57–65
  social, 5–8, 10, 14, 25, 67, 77–95
  verbal, 36–55
  utterance linkage, 33, 34, 37, 38, 49, 61–64, 71, 74
Context constraints, 48, 80
Context effects, 21, 22, 35, 36, 42, 46, 67, 71
Context events, 33–36, 62, 71
Contextual modification, 10, 11
Core meaning, 22, 23
Cumulative decoding, 111, 112, 123, 128

Decoding process, 10, 11, 14, 23, 29, 31–36, 53, 79, 91–94
Decoding strategy, 109–111, 113, 123, 124, 127, 128, 131, 143
Deep structure, 5, 13
Deitic words, 15, 16, 33
Denotative meaning, 78, 80
Descending adjective order, 112, 114–119, 121, 129
Designatum, 97, 98
Determination, 86, 87, 91